Introducing the New Geography **INTRODUCING URBAN STRUCTURE**

K BRIGGS BA
Senior Geography Master
Canon Slade School, Bolton

Hodder and Stoughton
London Sydney Auckland Toronto

The photograph on the cover is a view of part
of the city of Vancouver in British Columbia.
It will be found useful when studying the land
use patterns of Vancouver in chapters 5 and 8.
(The photograph is reproduced by courtesy of
the Government of British Columbia.)

ISBN 0 340 20254 8

First published 1977
Reprinted 1980

Produced in Great Britain for
Hodder and Stoughton Educational,
a division of Hodder and Stoughton Ltd,
Mill Road, Dunton Green, Sevenoaks, Kent,
by Bucken Ltd

Printed in Great Britain by
Biddles Ltd, Guildford, Surrey

Bibliography

For further study of the internal structure of urban areas the reader is referred to the following more advanced works:

Traffic in Towns: the specially shortened edition of the Buchanan Report, Penguin Books, 1964

BURKE, G. *Towns in the Making,* Arnold, 1971

CARTER, H. *The Study of Urban Geography,* Arnold, 1972

GOODALL, B. *The Economics of Urban Areas,* Pergamon Press, 1972

MAYER, H. M. and KOHN, C. F. (eds) *Readings in Urban Geography,* University of Chicago Press, 1959

SCOTT, P. *Geography and Retailing,* Hutchinson University Library, 1970

Preface

This book, the third in the 'Introducing the New Geography' series is concerned with the patterns of settlement, functions and movement found within urban areas. Like the two earlier books in the series (*Introducing Transportation Networks* and *Introducing Towns and Cities*) it uses a concept-based, problem-solving approach to geography, which is appropriate to modern thinking in the subject. Though it is designed primarily to be used by children in the 11 to 14 age-group, it will also be found useful as an introductory text for older and more advanced students. Emphasis is laid throughout upon personal investigation and analysis rather than on the arid learning of second-hand descriptions. Techniques are explained which permit the student to carry out successful research projects of his own. This will be found particularly valuable to teachers in view of present trends towards basing external examinations partly upon individual studies carried out by candidates. The Workbook provides a graded series of practical exercises which form a sound introduction to individual research work.

K. BRIGGS

Acknowledgements

Information on the shopping centre of Blackpool and Sheffield is derived from *Atlas of Major Suburban Shopping Centres*, D. Thorpe and C. J. Thomas, Retail Outlets Research Unit, Manchester Business School, 1971. Information on land-use characteristics in Vancouver is used with the permission of the City of Vancouver Planning Department. Information on land values in Vancouver is used with the permission of the Real Estate Board of Greater Vancouver. Information on the national origins of the population of Regina and the socio-economic patterns of Halifax were obtained from Cenours of Canada, 1971, with the permission of Statistics Canada. Several maps were derived from Ordnance Survey maps and the map extracts are reproduced with the sanction of the Controller of H.M. Stationery Office, Crown Copyright reserved. Various material was derived from census statistics as follows: population data, *Preliminary Report, 1971 Census; Car Availability, 1971 Census; Sample Census, 1966*; data relating to shops, *Census of Distributions, 1961*, al HMSO, London. Information on Oxford Street shops is derived from a map published by Chas. E. Good, Ltd., London.

Contents

Preface   *page* 3

Bibliography   *page* 3

Acknowledgements   *page* 4

1   **The Origin and Growth of Towns**   *page* 7
The formation of settlement clusters   *page* 7
Early towns in Britain   *page* 9
The modern expansion of towns   *page* 10

2   **Patterns of Urban Growth**   *page* 11
The process of growth   *page* 11
Urban growth in south-west London and Greater
Manchester   *page* 15
How to measure the shape of a town   *page* 16

3   **The Simulation of the Growth of a Town**   *page* 17
The building process   *page* 17
The weighting process   *page* 17
A 'run' of the simulation   *page* 20
An actual example: simulation of the growth of
Norwich   *page* 20

4   **The Texture of Towns**   *page* 23
Types of urban texture   *page* 23
The texture of Caernarvon   *page* 25

5   **Urban Functions : General Principles**   *page* 27
A simple concentric model   *page* 27
The simulation of a concentric pattern of urban land
use   *page* 29
More complex models   *page* 32
The land-use pattern of Vancouver   *page* 34

Contents

6 Shops and Offices   *page* 37
Convenience goods and shopping goods   *page* 37
A hierarchy of shopping centres   *page* 38
The composition of suburban shopping centres   *page* 38
Modern developments   *page* 40
Offices   *page* 40

7 The Central Business District   *page* 41
General characteristics of the central business district
page 41
Patterns of land use in the central business district   *page* 42

8 Industry and Residence   *page* 46
Industry   *page* 46
Residence   *page* 48

9 The Journey to Work   *page* 51
The journey to work in the Manchester area   *page* 51

10 Urban Movement and Planning   *page* 57
The town as a system   *page* 57
Conflict in urban movement   *page* 58
The planning of the urban environment   *page* 59

Human settlements (single buildings and groups of buildings) form widely differing patterns over the surface of the earth. In some places, single dwellings are scattered far apart; in others, buildings are arranged in small, compact groups to form hamlets and villages. Relatively large clusters of dwellings and other buildings form towns and cities. These types of settlement patterns are illustrated in figure 1.

In order to understand the characteristics of present-day towns, we must know something about the reasons why towns appeared in the first place, and also how they have grown, sometimes to an enormous size.

A THE FORMATION OF SETTLEMENT CLUSTERS

One of the problems which constantly faces people in their everyday lives is the difficulty of moving from place to place. Usually we live in one place and work, attend school, visit shops, or find our entertainment in quite different places. Hence, every day, we find ourselves frequently having to make journeys to satisfy our various wants. These journeys cost us time, money and effort, and usually the benefit only appears when the journey is completed. If we go on holiday by car we

often have to tolerate a long, uncomfortable trip, punctuated by annoying traffic jams. This difficulty of moving from place to place is called 'the friction of distance' or 'the friction of space'. In order to move about, we have to overcome a kind of friction which tends to hold us back.

In modern times, of course, much has been done to overcome the friction of distance. We can travel by train from Manchester to London in less time than it would take us to walk a dozen miles. An air journey across the Atlantic takes only a few hours. We can even overcome the friction of distance without actually travelling. By the use of a telephone we can be talking to friends or relatives on the Pacific coast of Canada in less than a minute.

figure 1 Settlement patterns

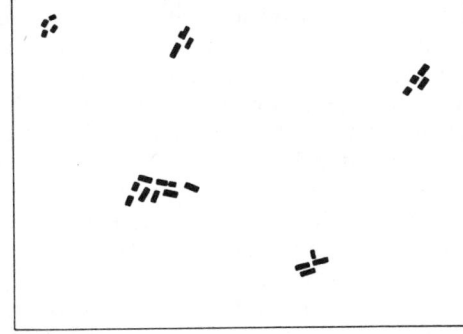

B Hamlets and villages

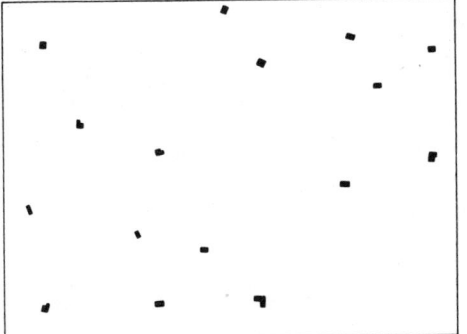

A Scattered single dwellings

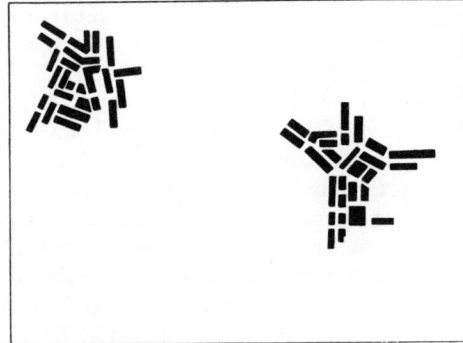

C Towns

Not so long ago however, when journeys could only be made on horseback, in horse-drawn vehicles or on foot, the friction of distance was a great barrier to movement. In those circumstances, people would try to arrange that they did as little travelling as possible.

Let us consider an area of land in which, long ago, the people worked as subsistence farmers, that is, each household satisfied its day-to-day needs by what it could produce from its particular patch of farmland. The friction of distance was very strong, most movement being on foot. A reasonably efficient form of settlement pattern might be the one shown in figure 2A. Houses are widely scattered, and each is located near the centre of its piece of farmland. People live as near to their work as possible, so that very little time or effort is wasted in travelling to work (i.e. in overcoming the friction of distance). No large settlement clusters can be formed. The unit of settlement is the single, isolated building.

An alternative settlement pattern is shown in figure 2B. In this case, the subsistence farmers live in houses grouped close together so as to form small village clusters. Each household's farmland is not a compact block, but consists of small strips of land scattered over the fields surrounding the village. Because these strips are so scattered, to have a house in the central village is the best way to reduce travelling to a minimum. But this village could never grow into a large town because, if there were more households in the village, the area of farmland would have to be greater, and households would have to

figure 2 The friction of distance

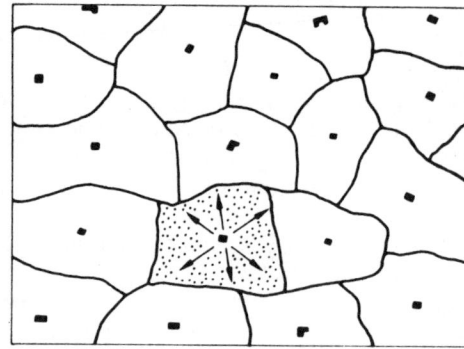

A Scattered houses

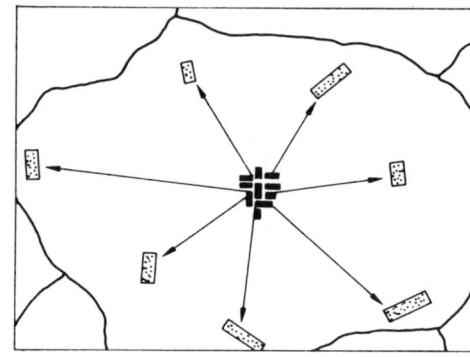

C Large village cluster

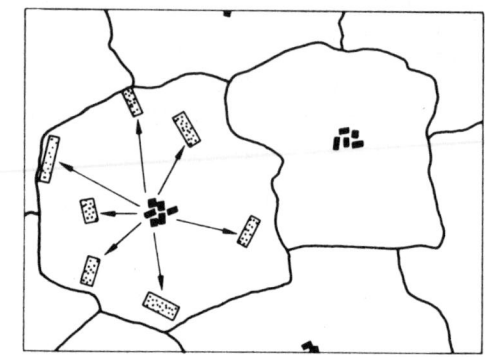

B Small village cluster

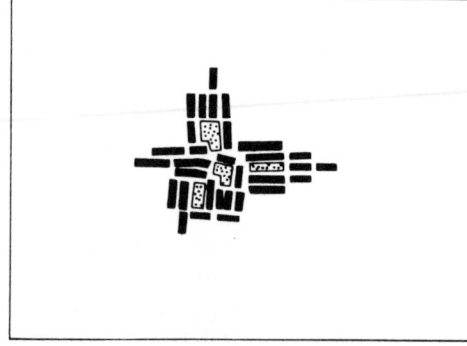

D Town

Key   ■ Dwelling

▨ Workplace

make long, wasteful journeys to cultivate their strips (fig. 2C).

People who live in towns do not often earn their living as farmers so, before towns can exist in an area, the farmers have to be able to produce enough to satisfy their own needs and, in addition, a surplus to support the townspeople. A market would be set up in the town, to which farmers would travel to buy and sell goods. The townspeople would also provide other services, such as entertainment, for the farming households in the surrounding area. If the friction of distance was very strong (i.e. movement was slow and difficult) there would have to be a great many of these small market towns, so that each was fairly near to its dependent farms and villages (fig. 3A). As transport improved, and the friction of distance became weaker, market towns could be bigger and spaced further apart (fig. 3B).

The inhabitants of these towns would find their work in the towns themselves. Instead of the workplace being a large area of farmland, it could be a single building in which a number of householders found work. Thus, dwellings and buildings used as workplaces could be located very close together, forming a cluster of settlement much larger than a village (fig. 2D). Later, when large factories appeared, a great many households could reduce the friction of distance by living as near to these workplaces as possible.

Thus, with the development of non-farming economic activities, while transport facilities were relatively poor, there was a great tendency for people to cluster together in towns. Many workplaces concerned with industry and commerce were set up in advantageous positions, and residences gathered near these workplaces so that people could easily walk to work.

Another reason for the formation of clusters of urban settlement in the past was the need for defence. A population scattered thinly over the countryside in single households or small villages could not defend itself from attack. Hence, in times and places in which there was a serious danger of being attacked, people tended to cluster together and create a town which could be surrounded by a defensive wall. Such towns were often set up in places where the natural landscape provided some measure of defence, using a river as a natural moat for example.

B EARLY TOWNS IN BRITAIN

A few towns existed in Britain in Roman times but, with the Saxon invasions of the fifth century, town life declined and was replaced by a subsistence farming economy based upon villages. Roman towns, like Chester, Lincoln and York, declined, in some cases never to recover. In the eighth century, the Norse invasions stimulated town development, particularly in eastern England, at places such as Derby, Leicester and Nottingham. In the eleventh century, following the Norman invasion, castles were set up at strategic locations and, as a result, some villages grew into towns. Other villages gained the right, commonly in the fourteenth and fifteenth centuries, to hold a market or

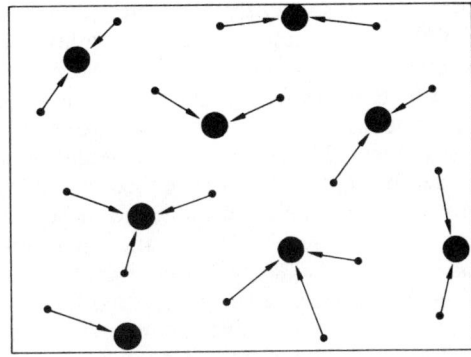

A With strong friction of distance

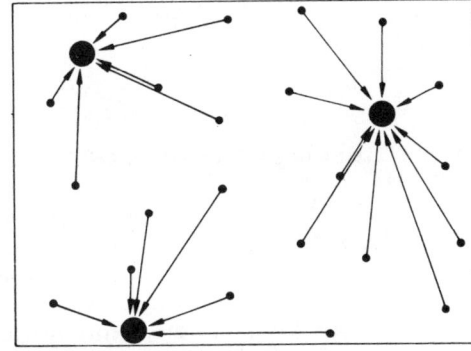

B With weaker friction of distance

Key

 Market town
• Village

figure 3 The spacing of market towns

a fair, and consequently grew into towns. In addition, many 'new towns' were created in medieval times. At least forty of these were set up in the hundred years following 1066, many in locations where no earlier town had existed. New Towns of the thirteenth and fourteenth centuries were called bastides. Examples include New Winchelsea in Sussex, Kingston-upon-Hull (Hull) and Berwick-upon-Tweed. Also, at this time, Edward I set up bastides to defend the conquered lands of North Wales. Thus, Flint, Beaumaris, Caernarvon, Conway and others came into existence. With the coming of the Industrial Revolution and factory industry, many other towns grew, particularly in the north and the Midlands, sometimes built around the nucleus of a medieval village.

C THE MODERN EXPANSION OF TOWNS

As industries developed on a large scale in the nineteenth century, many people moved from the countryside into the growing urban areas to seek work in the factories. Thus towns came to have closely packed areas of residential settlement in close proximity to workplaces. These areas of terraced houses can be seen in most British towns.

During the nineteenth century however, improvements in transport began to make great reductions in the friction of distance. Railways developed in the 1830s, and by 1850 the greater part of the pattern had been created. The bicycle appeared in the 1880s, electric tramcars in the 1890s, and motor buses in the early twentieth century. The mass use of motor cars really began in the 1920s. Since then, the friction of distance has been further reduced by the introduction of telephones, radio and television, which to some extent make journeys unnecessary.

All these developments have allowed residences to be located at some distance from workplaces. Hence, it has become less necessary to concentrate urban functions in small areas, as in early towns. The growing urban populations have moved outwards towards the edge of the town, and the surrounding farmland has gradually become urbanized. Despite the fact that, in most towns, the greatest concentration of workplaces is found in the town centre, it has become possible for people to live several miles away in the suburbs, and make daily journeys to work. This process has been called 'the urban explosion'; towns have 'exploded' into the surrounding countryside.

As individual towns have expanded in this way, sometimes they have joined up with one another to form a conurbation, a very large, almost continuously built-up area which originally had several separate urban nuclei. The Greater London, West Midland, Greater Manchester and West Yorkshire conurbations are British examples. In north-eastern USA a further development has taken place, by which the Boston, New York, Philadelphia, Baltimore and Washington conurbations have themselves expanded to form a super conurbation which is sometimes referred to as Megalopolis.

It has even been suggested that, in the future, cities, which came into existence through the need for people to live near their work and to have close contact with one another, may become unnecessary, at least in the form in which we know them now. Enormous reductions in the restriction of distance through the development of high-speed transport systems, television, easy long-distance telephone contacts (STD) and access to computer data processing and storage systems may result in a scattering of settlement away from traditional urban nuclei, possibly to create a world-wide urbanized area. The name Ecumenopolis (universal city) has been suggested.

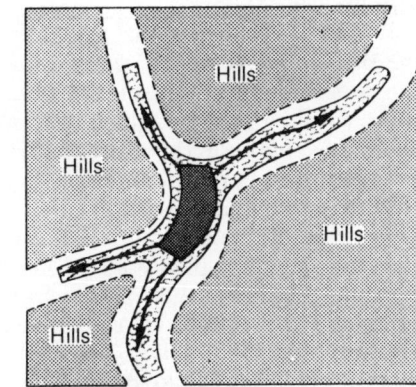

A

B

C

D

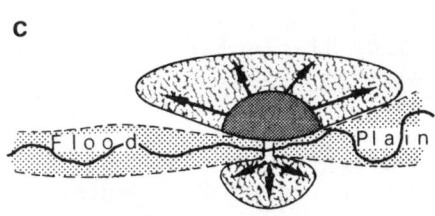

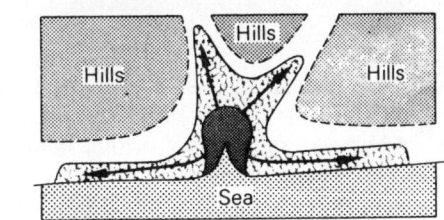

figure 4 Physical influences on urban growth patterns

Chapter Two
Patterns of Urban Growth

We have seen in Chapter One, that in the nineteenth and twentieth centuries towns have expanded rapidly around their original nuclei. If a town was surrounded by a perfectly uniform land surface over which to expand, we would expect it to grow concentrically outwards like ripples spread outwards in a pond (fig. 4A). In fact, of course, the land surface is not perfectly uniform. In some directions it presents obstacles to urban expansion; in others it encourages expansion. It is therefore rare to find a town with a straight or gently curving boundary. Usually the edge of the built-up area has advanced to form lobes in some areas, and has remained static in others. The overall shape of a town has been influenced partly by physical factors and partly by human factors.

A THE PROCESS OF GROWTH

a) Physical Factors

In an upland area, towns tend to expand along the valley floors, thus avoiding the building and other problems set by steep, valleyside slopes (fig. 4B). Sometimes however, since the earliest expansion in the nineteenth century involved the better-off people, a hilly area commanding attractive views would be developed to create a rather exclusive suburb. Later, though, the line of least resistance along the valley floor would be taken for less expensive housing.

In low-lying areas, river flood plains have tended to be bypassed and left undeveloped (fig. 4C). Rivers have often acted as barriers to growth because they are usually crossed by only a few bridges. Hence, it is common to find that a riverside town has developed to a greater extent on one bank of a river than on the other (fig. 4C).

Coastal towns, perhaps originating in a cluster around a harbour, have tended to develop inland along valleys, and laterally along the coast, particularly for residential areas, so as to gain the advantage of proximity to the sea (fig. 4D). Coastal towns are almost inevitably asymmetrically shaped simply because they are not able to expand seawards.

b) Human Factors

Perhaps the most important human factors influencing the pattern of urban growth are related to the sequence of the development of transport facilities in the town and its surrounding area.

1 Canals have provided bulk transport facilities since very early times and have therefore tended to attract industrial enterprises which use bulky raw materials. In a cruise through a town along a canal, one usually sees a monotonous succession of old factories and warehouses, often in a poor state of repair. The banks of canals, therefore, did attract industrial settlement. But canals, like rivers, usually have few bridges, and the ones that exist are often narrow and

hump-backed. Hence, canals have often acted as barriers to urban expansion. The tide of settlement would often come to a halt at the line of the canal, moving across it only at bridges (fig. 5A).

2 By the 1830s when the railways came, some British towns were already quite large, so it was thought desirable to locate the station within the area which was already built up. In some cases therefore, railway lines penetrated these early urban areas by the use of viaducts to avoid closing existing streets. In other cases tunnels were used, particularly if the route of the railway lay along a low-lying valley floor. In other places, large areas of dilapidated property were demolished to make way for the railway (fig. 5B). Rival railway companies would often set up their stations in a ring around the central part of the built-up area, as in London.

In smaller towns the station would commonly be located at the edge of the built-up area of the time (fig. 5C) and the line would either bypass the town or tunnel beneath it, so as to avoid unnecessary demolition. But people in those days were not so conscious of the importance of 'environment' as they are today. At Conway, in North Wales, for example, the railway was driven through a corner of the ancient walled town.

In the case of very small towns the railway, intended to link larger towns together, did not deviate from its route to approach the town. Hence the station could be located a mile or more outside the built-up area of the time. This could later cause the town to expand in the direction of the station (fig. 5D).

Some towns (Crewe, Redhill and Swindon, for example) were almost entirely created by

the railway. Swindon, in 1831, was a small market town with a population of under 2000. The arrival of the railway and the establishment of a railway works in the 1840s led to a rapid increase in population—to over 50 000 by the early twentieth century.

Once in existence, the railways greatly reduced the friction of distance. They allowed towns to grow by making it possible for people to make longer journeys to the town centre. But, since trains can only be boarded at stations, urban growth was limited at first to a small area around each station (fig. 5E), especially since most people had to walk to the station. Later, as tramcars and buses appeared, it became easier to reach suburban stations, so the clusters of urban settlement around the stations expanded to produce a continuous corridor of settlement (fig. 5E). This process commonly occurred in the London suburbs, especially in those to the south of the Thames. Even nowadays, when car ownership is widespread, suburban stations keep their function. People now often drive to the station, park the car there and ride by train into central London.

Railways have also had a negative effect on urban expansion. Since it was desirable to have as few bridges as possible, railways became linear barriers to urban growth, like rivers and canals. A railway line could guide the growth of the town in certain directions or it could temporarily dam urban expansion (fig. 5C).

3 The growing town usually inherited a radial system of roads, but in the early nineteenth century the friction of distance was very great. Later, however, with improvements in road transport, the road pattern

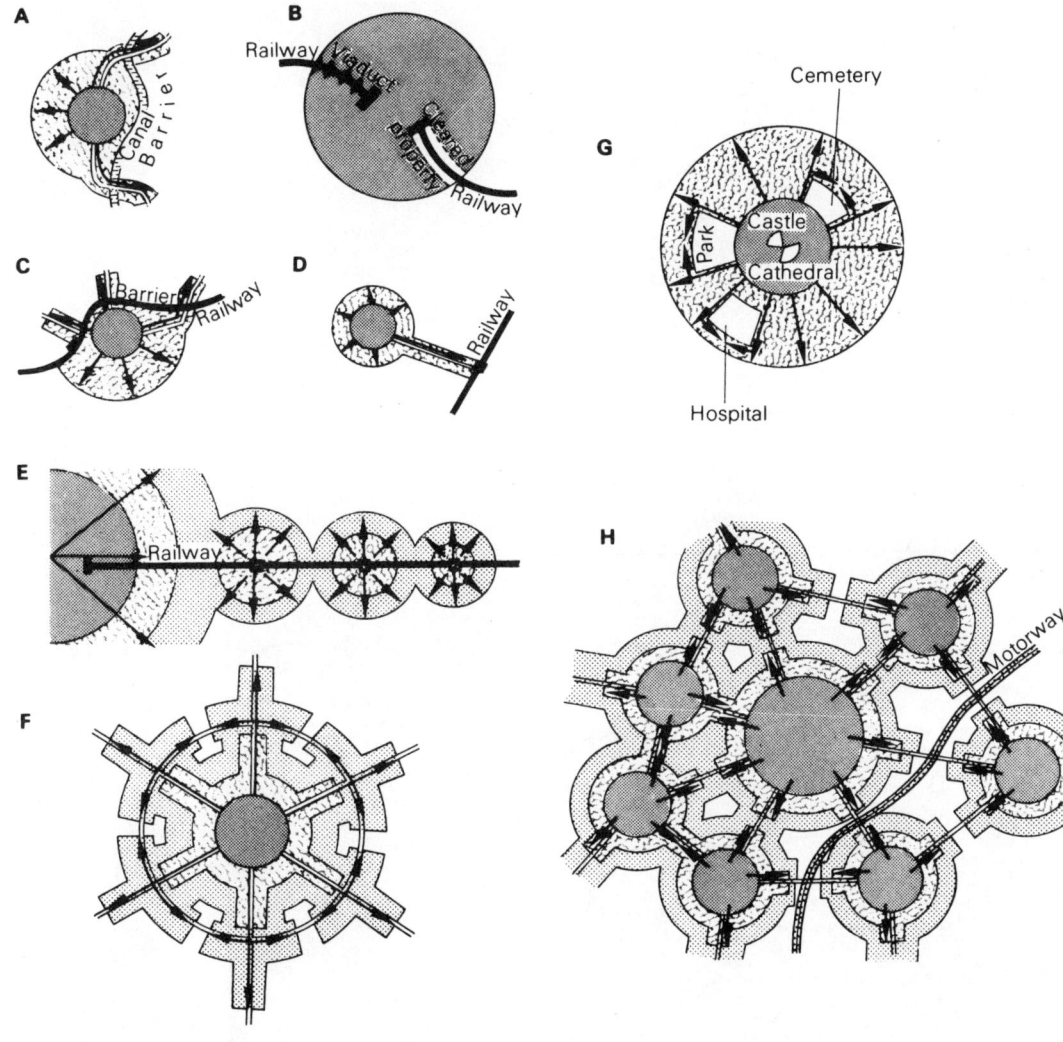

figure 5 Human influences on urban growth patterns

came to have an important influence on the pattern of urban growth. Tramcar routes were usually established predominantly along these radial roads and early bus routes followed the same pattern. The effect was that the early urban nucleus thrust out tentacles of settlement along the radial roads (fig. 5F), resulting in the creation of a star-shaped town. Ribbon development of this kind saved the cost of building new roads and made it easy to supply utilities such as water and gas mains.

The coming of the motor car and motor lorry meant that transport became much more flexible. Easy movement was no longer restricted to the radial roads. Also many ring roads were built around the circumference of the town. Thus the infilling of the spaces between the radial lobes of settlement could take place (fig. 5F). But the use of cars and lorries, unlike that of tramcars and buses, means that space has to be provided for parking when people have completed their journeys. This was an added encouragement for urban activities to move to areas of plentiful land on the outskirts of the town.

Urban motorways have usually been built through areas which have remained unused during the town's expansion (fig. 5H), so as to reduce demolition to a minimum, though in some cases they have been directed through former areas of old property. In many ways the urban motorway is similar to the railway. It provides accessibility only at the entry points, which are therefore similar to stations. A motorway also is at least as effective a barrier to urban expansion as a railway line, so the pattern of urban motorways may have a great influence on future urban growth patterns.

4 The introduction of the widespread use of electricity as an industrial power supply has given industry a much greater flexibility of choice of location within the town. Industrial undertakings no longer need to be clustered in particular parts of the town. They have therefore been able to move outwards and take their part in urban expansion.

5 In spite of the importance of the outward growth of the town, we must not forget that many open spaces, often of considerable size, survive within the town's built-up area. These are often devoted to special functions. In the ancient town nucleus there may be open spaces surrounding a castle or a cathedral, many of them now used as car parks. The commons of the London area have been protected legally from becoming built over since the middle of the nineteenth century, and other cities such as Southampton and Newcastle-upon-Tyne have similar areas. As towns grew in the nineteenth century, many parks and cemeteries were laid out, often on vacant land near the edge of the town at the time. These Queen's Parks and Victoria Parks can be approximately dated by their very names. These of course, once in existence, represented barriers to urban growth, and the expanding town was forced to move like a tide around these 'islands' (fig. 5G).

6 As a result of all the processes explained above, in some parts of Britain, fairly closely spaced towns have expanded, especially along the roads, to create very large conurbations (fig. 5H). The existence of this modern kind of urban settlement has been recognized by the government in the 1974 reorganization

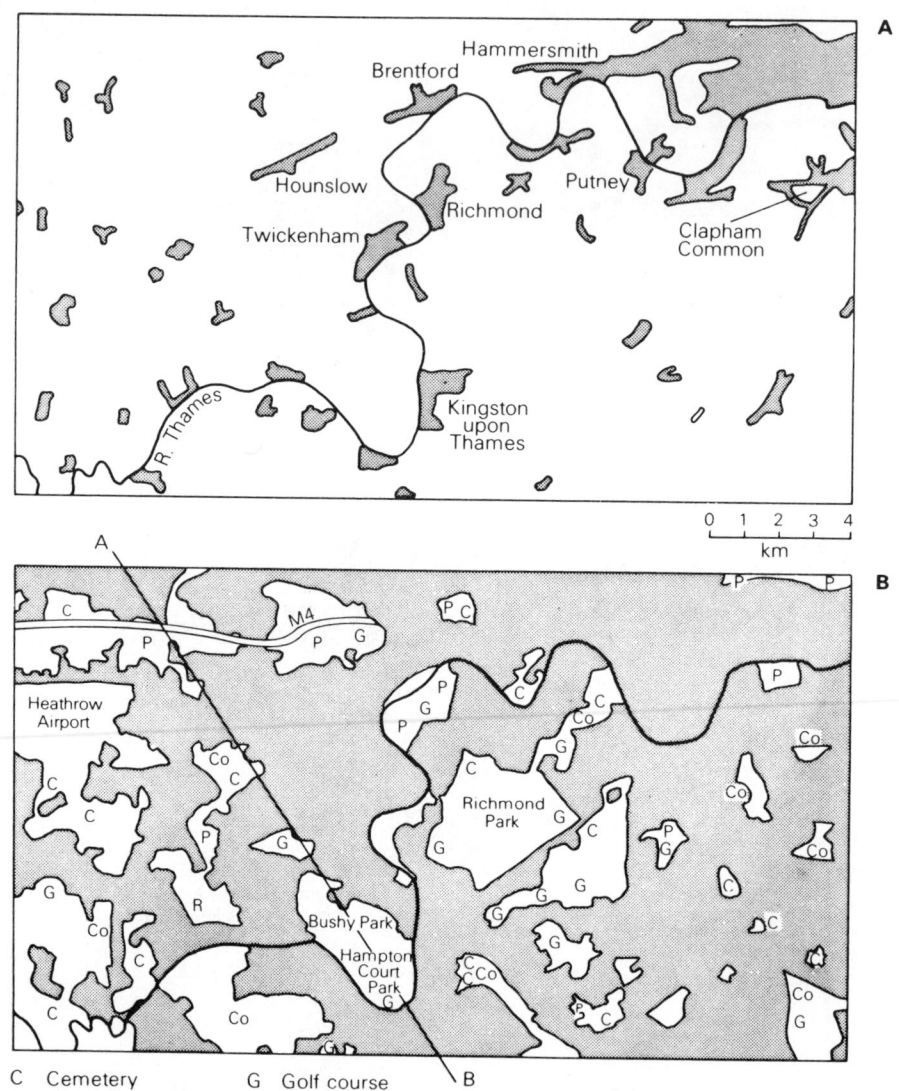

C Cemetery   G Golf course
Co Common or Heath R Race course
P Park

figure 6 Urban growth in south-west London

of local government units. It is thought desirable to treat conurbations such as Greater Manchester, the West Midlands and West Yorkshire as single units for some local government purposes. In effect, each conurbation is being regarded to some extent as a single large city. The Greater London conurbation of course has a longer history.

B   URBAN GROWTH IN SOUTH WEST LONDON AND GREATER MANCHESTER

The growth of a conurbation is well illustrated by the expansion of London towards the south-west since the middle of the nineteenth century (fig. 6A and B). The open space in the north-east corner of each of the maps in figure 6 contains Buckingham Palace and St. James' Park. In the mid-nineteenth century, lobes from the built-up area of London extended as far as Hammersmith to the north of the Thames, and Clapham Common to the south, which had been enclosed by a narrow strip of settlement. Hounslow and the riverside settlements of Putney, Brentford, Richmond, Twickenham and Kingston were still quite separate from London, and there were many villages to the west and south. Figure 6B shows that London's expansion has engulfed all the settlements named above, but many open spaces are still left, large ones such as Richmond Park, Wimbledon Common, Bushy Park and Hampton Court Park, as well as Heathrow Airport, and smaller ones such as Clapham Common. In addition to being used as parks, these urban open

figure 7 Urban growth in the northern part of Greater Manchester

spaces contain golf courses, cemeteries and a race course (Kempton Park). The M4 motorway is directed as far as possible along fairly open country, but near Brentford it enters the built-up area. Since the process which has taken place here is predominantly the south-westward expansion of London, the density of urban settlement decreases generally from north-east to south-west. This is made clear when one is drawing the map. South-west of line AB the map is most easily drawn by outlining the built-up areas; north-east of the line by outlining the open spaces.

South-west London contrasts to some extent with the northern part of the Greater Manchester conurbation (fig. 7). This area is much less continuously built up. Bolton, Bury and Rochdale can still be identified as separate towns. This is not so much an example of the expansion of Manchester as of the expansion of each of the separate units of the conurbation, so that they have become linked together by urbanized strips of varying width. Over practically the whole area, in drawing the map, one outlines the built-up areas rather than the open spaces. The M61, M62 and M63, and other roads of motorway standard have found it relatively easy to find space between the major urban clusters.

C HOW TO MEASURE THE SHAPE OF A TOWN

It is quite easy to measure the length and breadth of a town's built-up area in kilometres or miles simply by using a ruler and a map. No really accurate way of measuring a town's *shape* exists, partly because there are no simple units to use for measurement. We shall use a method which measures approximately how much a town's shape differs from a circle. The procedure is as follows.

1 Draw the outer edge of the built-up area of the town, omitting outlying villages but including cemeteries and parks which are completely surrounded by buildings.

2 Find the centre of gravity of the built-up area. This can be done by tracing its outline on a piece of thin cardboard and carefully cutting out the shape with scissors. This shape is then balanced on a compass point.

3 Draw a line through the centre of gravity running as nearly as possible along the town's longest axis. Then draw three other lines, also passing through the centre of gravity so that eight 45-degree angles are formed around the centre of gravity.

This procedure has been carried out in figure 8 for the built-up area of Southport in about 1964. Each radial line from the centre of gravity has been allocated a number. The calculation is then carried out as follows. Refer to the table in figure 8.

Column (1): This lists the distance in kilometres (though any other units may be used) along each radial line from the centre of gravity to the edge of the built-up area. The sum of all these distances is given at the foot of the column.

Column (2): Here the length of each radial is given as a percentage of the sum of all eight distances.

Column (3): This shows what the percentage length of each radial would be if Southport were perfectly circular in shape. In a circle, of course, all radii are equal in length.

Column (4): Each figure is the difference between Columns (2) and (3). The sum of these differences (53.8) indicates by how much Southport's shape differs from that of a circle.

Clearly, Southport's shape differs very greatly from a circle. The town appears to have expanded parallel to the coast along the A565(T) road. It might be interesting to investigate why it has not grown in a similar way along the A570.

This method of measuring shape will give slightly different results according to the precise orientation chosen for the radials. This is inevitable in such a simple method. More accurate results can be obtained by increasing the number of radials, but of course this increases the amount of calculation needed.

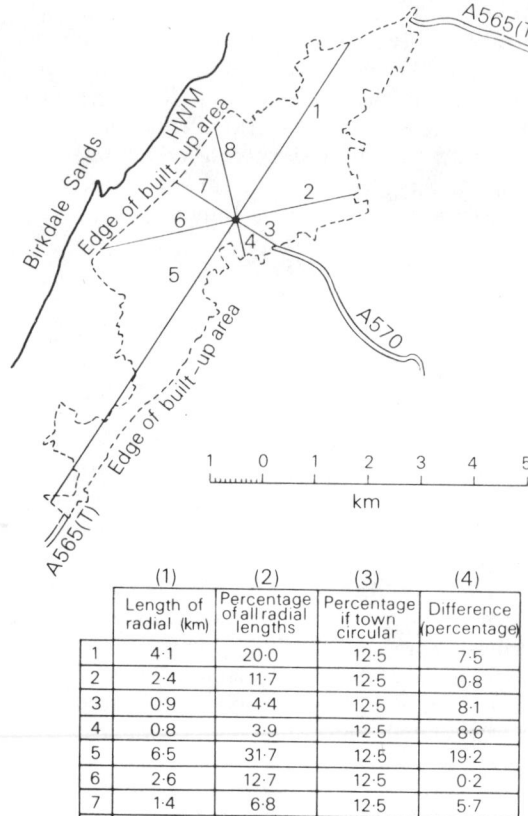

(1)	(2)	(3)	(4)
	Length of radial (km)	Percentage of all radial lengths	Percentage if town circular	Difference (percentage)
1	4·1	20·0	12·5	7·5
2	2·4	11·7	12·5	0·8
3	0·9	4·4	12·5	8·1
4	0·8	3·9	12·5	8·6
5	6·5	31·7	12·5	19·2
6	2·6	12·7	12·5	0·2
7	1·4	6·8	12·5	5·7
8	1·8	8·8	12·5	3·7
Total	20·5	100·0	100·0	53·8

Shape index = 53·8

figure 8 The measurement of a town's shape—Southport about 1964

In Chapter Two we have examined various physical and human factors which may have influenced the growth patterns of particular towns. We shall now learn how to conduct an experiment in town building. We shall begin with the nucleus of the town in the middle of the nineteenth century and, by allowing these various factors to operate, we shall simulate the town's growth over 100 to 150 years to its present form. In this way, we may come to understand urban growth processes a little better. The method is explained below.

A THE BUILDING PROCESS

The town will be built on a 10×10 set of squares (fig. 9) instead of an ordinary map. We shall build the town one square at a time. You will see that, in figure 9, each square can be identified by two digits, one being an 'easting' and the other a 'northing', as on Ordnance Survey maps. The shaded square in figure 9A, for example, is square 65 (6 easting and 5 northing).

In the building process we shall allow as far as possible for the factors we think have influenced the town's growth, but we shall also introduce a 'chance' factor, which represents factors we might not know about, various unpredictable human decisions, etc.

This is done by using the table of random sampling numbers (Table I). In this table any number from 1 to 0 has an equal chance of appearing anywhere in the table. To begin to build, we choose a pair of digits anywhere in Table I and this pair of digits is used to score a 'hit' on the grid square which it represents. We then work, from here, either along the rows of the table or down the columns, taking each pair of digits in turn and scoring 'hits' on the appropriate squares. A single 'hit' will not usually cause a square to be built up; most will have to be hit a few times. When a square has been 'hit' the necessary number of times, it is shaded in to indicate that it is built up. Any further 'hits' on this square are ignored.

B THE WEIGHTING PROCESS

Because of the influence of physical and human factors on urban growth, some squares will be more likely to be built up than others. Hence each square is allocated a 'weight', a number which is marked in its top-left corner. This number represents the number of times the square has to be 'hit' before it is built up. The smaller the number, the greater the probability of the square becoming built up. As a 'hit' is scored on a particular square, this number is crossed out and replaced by a

number one unit less. Thus, if a square weighted 4 is 'hit', the 4 is crossed out and replaced by a 3. When a square weighted 1 is 'hit' it is immediately built up. The weighting of the squares is carried out by allowing for each physical or human factor in turn, as follows.

a) Proximity to the early nucleus

It seems reasonable to suppose that parts of the town nearer to the early nucleus are more likely to be built up than areas further away from it. Hence we insert gradually increasing weights in squares as we move away from the nucleus. Squares adjacent to (i.e. having a common side with) the early nucleus are given a weight of 1; the ones next further out are weighted as 2, and so on. This process has been carried out for the imaginary town in figure 9A, in which square 65 is the original nucleus.

b) Proximity to main roads

Because of the ease of movement along main roads we would expect areas of the town near main roads to be particularly likely to be built up. We allow for this factor in two stages.
1 The pattern of main roads in the area is shown in figure 9B. The procedure is now to begin at square 65 and follow each main road

TABLE I *Random sampling numbers for simulation of urban growth*

13	69	23	05	90	34	65	76	29	68	24	59	81	59	79	56	30	60	84	78
48	92	55	96	47	30	35	61	63	43	81	33	80	11	59	87	11	09	16	17
67	44	38	25	59	35	54	99	23	64	01	57	10	96	97	07	42	45	15	02
53	98	28	37	83	32	86	56	64	81	10	60	16	43	35	60	29	94	72	12
82	51	98	14	52	53	84	04	81	47	39	58	17	70	02	28	22	07	50	67
14	20	59	69	61	33	65	67	89	57	10	97	67	91	30	51	36·	41	24	64
28	92	71	66	83	78	36	33	26	19	60	12	48	36	92	19	52	65	14	62
20	26	22	31	82	20	39	03	57	07	28	95	15	32	96	63	84	46	52	20
73	54	27	55	88	93	76	46	09	66	00	61	16	92	06	37	97	02	65	18
75	95	93	91	43	71	07	90	99	65	11	98	52	43	98	00	30	13	03	87
80	15	61	77	83	78	38	61	27	92	04	63	93	74	58	80	99	77	90	51
13	68	20	94	61	13	38	85	87	72	70	89	52	33	74	47	90	91	56	36
89	21	88	14	21	08	34	86	77	94	01	45	82	33	35	03	76	38	05	40
63	36	40	15	85	34	39	05	30	37	88	29	35	83	38	06	05	67	18	37
95	21	99	41	73	73	34	11	70	51	57	74	49	57	84	08	51	15	88	69
73	50	38	37	55	39	35	62	12	96	44	16	10	05	03	85	90	18	13	66
99	42	18	67	17	53	75	11	98	84	99	70	07	25	84	82	69	10	66	57
93	10	65	26	41	41	90	04	15	69	66	63	31	64	49	17	69	21	50	60
14	76	50	59	72	20	68	86	73	80	19	75	32	74	50	25	81	22	51	19
76	58	28	76	46	94	02	40	17	95	54	56	83	32	97	21	47	79	92	13
45	62	01	87	84	05	06	39	52	76	45	60	98	86	45	42	94	00	35	88
92	69	48	48	26	60	68	72	88	71	74	14	84	80	53	37	01	88	71	25
31	51	63	58	77	62	34	06	97	01	76	73	97	44	98	33	48	27	83	11
41	66	42	08	57	24	62	38	39	30	12	21	28	87	41	96	28	12	03	73
23	77	34	42	21	88	65	66	56	51	09	83	45	82	99	43	06	63	22	98

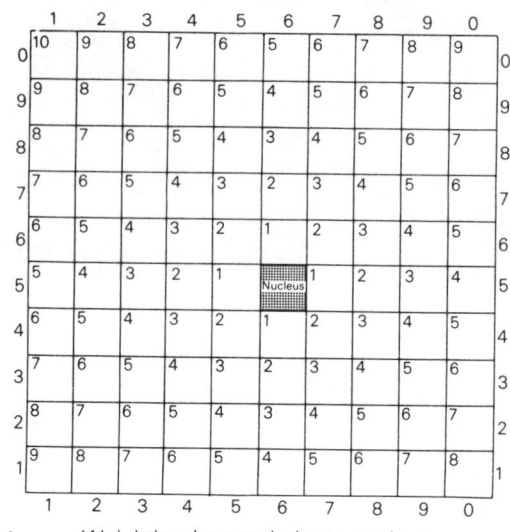

A Weighting by proximity to nucleus

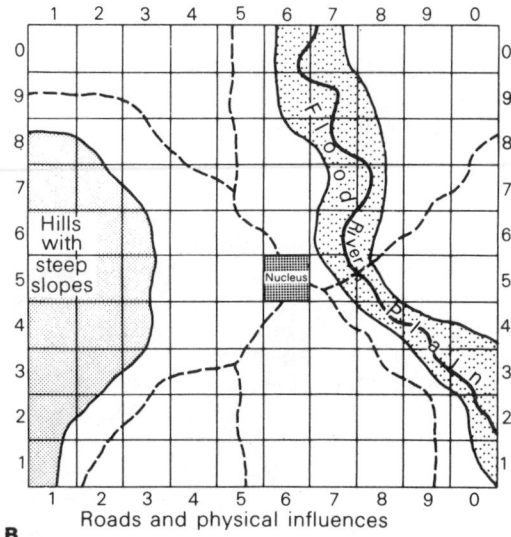

B Roads and physical influences

outwards, allocating new weights in the order 1, 1, 2, 2, 3, 3, 4, 4, etc. to each successive square the road passes through. All other squares keep the weighting as in figure 9A. Thus the 'main road squares' are given a higher probability of becoming built up. In most towns it is sufficient to take the 'A' class roads only for this purpose, but in others it may be better to include the 'B' class roads as well. The effect of this weighting process is shown in figure 9C.

2 The main roads would also give some degree of accessibility to the squares near the 'main road squares'. Hence, the squares in the spaces between the 'main road squares' should now be re-weighted in such a way that

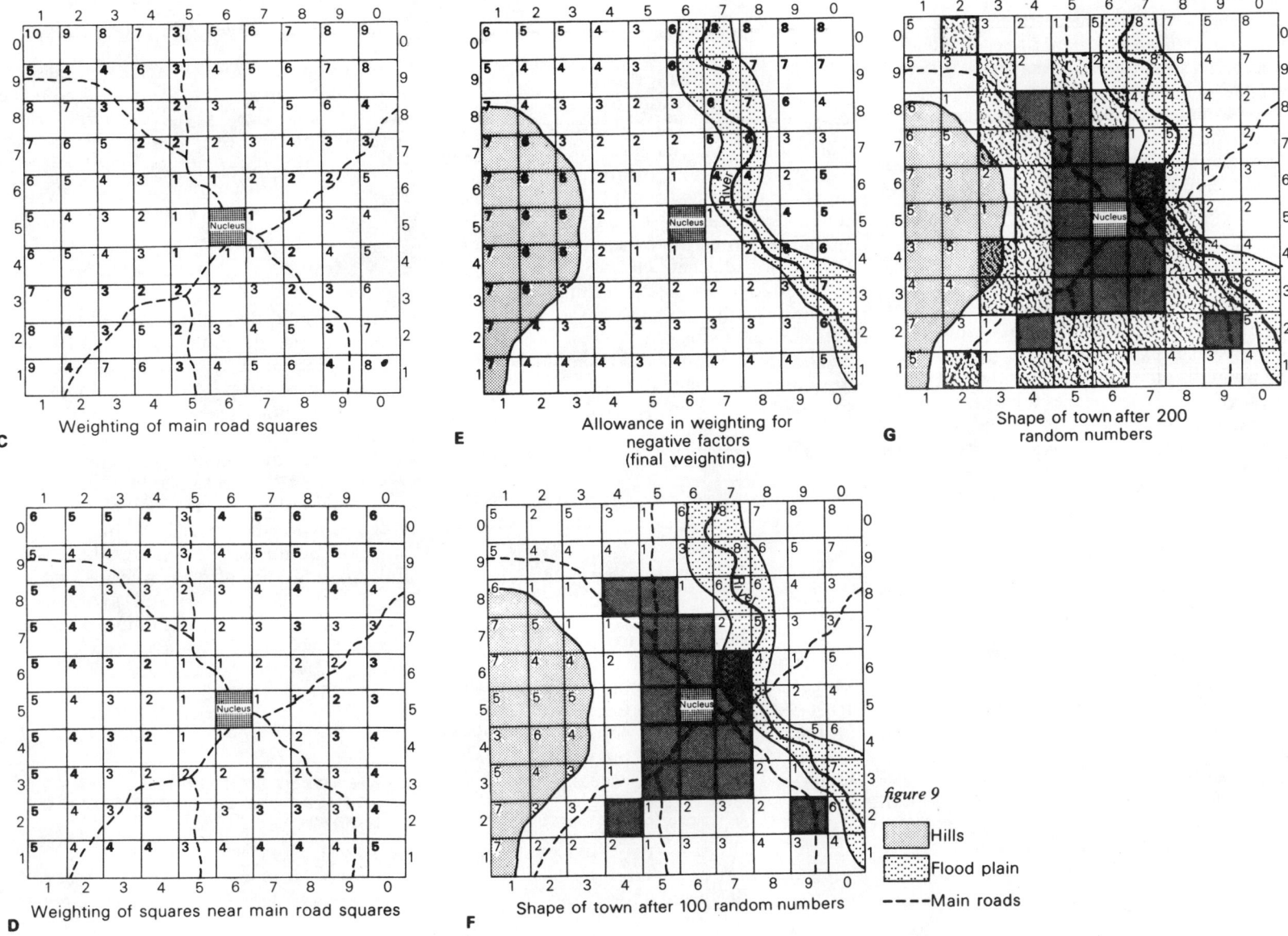

C — Weighting of main road squares

E — Allowance in weighting for negative factors (final weighting)

G — Shape of town after 200 random numbers

D — Weighting of squares near main road squares

F — Shape of town after 100 random numbers

figure 9

Hills

Flood plain

— — — Main roads

the weights increase successively by 1 away from the 'main road squares' to each adjacent square. If a square seems to have two different weights, the smaller one is taken. If a particular square has already been allocated a weight in figure 9A and C which is smaller than the one it would have by this process, it should keep the smaller weight. The result of doing this is shown in figure 9D.

c) The Influence of negative factors

We must finally make an allowance in weighting for various negative factors which may hinder urban expansion. As a general rule, the weight is increased by 2 for the first negative factor which influences the square and by an extra 1 for each of any other negative factors. Suggested negative factors include the following.

1 The square may be more than half occupied by high ground (select a particular contour line which you think may be important in the particular case).

2 There may be particularly steep slopes in the square.

3 More than half of the square may be occupied by an area of flood plain.

4 The square may be located on the opposite side of a river from the early nucleus, but this factor should not be applied to the 'main road cells'.

In particular simulation studies, other negative factors may be recognized in addition to these.

Figure 9E shows the final pattern of weights after allowance has been made for negative factors.

d) The 'momentum' effect

As the town grows, the outer boundary of its built-up area gradually extends outwards, and new building generally takes place at this outer boundary. Thus a former rural area will gradually become more likely to be built over as the expanding frontier of urbanization moves nearer to it. To allow for this 'momentum' effect, during the simulation, a 'hit' should be scored in any square which comes to have *two* adjacent (sharing a common side) built-up squares. The building up of each succeeding adjacent square scores an extra 'hit' on the square.

These rather complicated simulation 'rules' are summarized in Table II.

TABLE II   *Summary of the weighting process*

a) From the early nucleus, give successively greater weights (1, 2, 3, 4, etc) to adjacent squares moving outwards.

b) **1** Weight the 'main road squares' successively 1, 1, 2, 2, 3, 3, 4, 4, etc away from the early nucleus.

2 Weight other squares away from 'main road squares' by consecutively higher weights, so that there is never a difference greater than 1 between adjacent squares.

c) Increase weights of squares affected by negative factors. Add 2 for the first negative factor and 1 for each succeeding one in any square.

d) During simulation, score a 'hit' on any square which gains two adjacent built-up squares, and an extra 'hit' for each additional adjacent built-up square.

Instead of weighting the negative factors exactly as in (c) in Table II, it is quite possible to substitute a graduated scale for these, if preferred. For example, a weight of 1 could be given for land over, say, 100 metres, and a further 1 for land over 200 metres. In fact, many variations of detail are possible within the overall simulation method.

C A 'RUN' OF THE SIMULATION

Figure 9F and G illustrate a 'run' of the simulation for the imaginary town under discussion. Figure 9F illustrates the position after the use of 100 pairs of random numbers. Seventeen squares have been built up, mostly around the early nucleus, but also tending to extend north and south along the corridor between the hills and the flood plain. Square 76, a flood plain square, has already been built up. After the use of a further hundred pairs of numbers, 42 squares have been built up, in addition to the nucleus (fig. 9G). In general, the town is still avoiding the negative areas, but it is beginning to advance into the hills (square 34) and eastwards across the river and the flood plain, via the road (square 85).

D AN ACTUAL EXAMPLE: SIMULATION OF THE GROWTH OF NORWICH

The city of Norwich is easily contained within an area 10 km by 10 km. Hence, in this

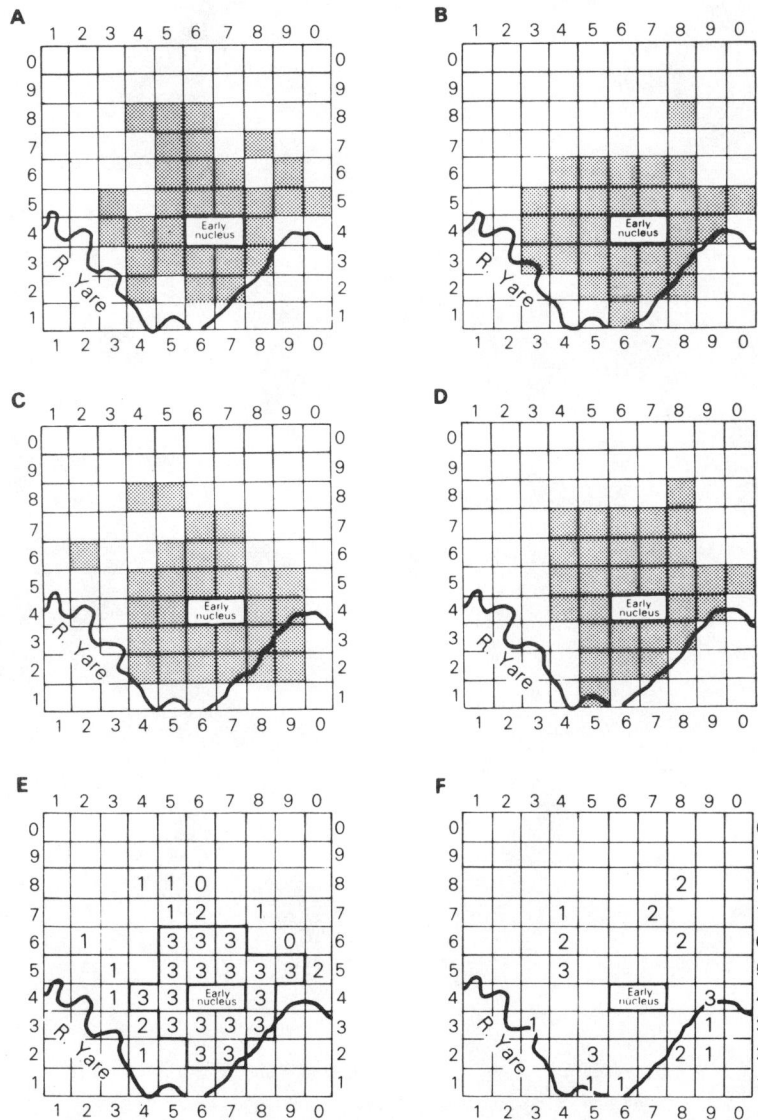

simulation, the squares used are the 1 sq km grid squares, as on Ordnance Survey maps. The early nucleus of the city comprises squares 64 and 74 (fig. 10). In weighting, distance from this early nucleus and all A and B class roads have been taken into account. There are no serious relief problems in the area, and nowhere is there a flood plain wide enough to occupy half of a grid square. The river Yare, to the south of the city (fig. 10) has been regarded as a barrier to southward expansion. Hence, squares to the south of the river have been given a negative weighting of 2. The Yare's north bank tributary, the Wensum, has not been regarded as a barrier because it actually passes through the city's early nucleus.

The existing built-up area of Norwich is shown in figure 10A, and three different 'runs' of the simulation, using the same weights, are illustrated in figures 10B, C and D. In general there is a close similarity between the simulations and the real city; all three simulations correctly indentify over 20 of the 30 built-up squares. This seems to suggest that the factors selected for weighting have not had a negligible influence on the shape of the city. Figure 10E summarizes the success of the three simulations. All three correctly build up seventeen squares fairly near the early nucleus; in the surrounding area they are less

figure 10 Simulation of the growth of Norwich.
A—actual pattern of built-up squares in Norwich.
B—first run of simulation. C—second run of simulation.
D—third run of simulation. E—number of times
actual built-up squares are correctly identified by the
simulations. F—number of times empty spaces were
incorrectly built up by the simulations

successful. In figure 10F it can be seen that certain squares tend to become built-up during the simulations and yet are not built-up in reality. It is interesting to look a little more closely at these.

Squares 68 and 96 (fig. 10E), weighted 3 and 2 respectively, into which settlement has recently extended, are not built-up in any of the simulations. On the other hand, in all three simulations, squares 45, 52 and 94 are built-up (fig. 10F) incorrectly. From maps it is not easy to explain why settlement has not come to dominate these squares, though there is an area of flood plain in two of them. Other squares one is rather surprised to find 'empty' are 86, which contains a large part of Mouse-hold Heath, 46, and 82, which is very near the city centre in spite of lying mostly to the south of the Yare (fig. 10A). In general, it appears that Norwich has expanded rather less than might have been expected towards the north-east and south-east, along the radial roads in those directions.

As towns have evolved through the centuries they have not only acquired particular overall shapes and patterns of open spaces, they have also come to possess areas with different *textures*. In some parts of a town the texture may be 'fine-grained' with lots of small buildings divided by an intricate network of narrow streets. In others, it may be 'coarse-grained' with large buildings and very few streets. The texture of a town is to a great extent the existing record of the town's evolution. At some times in the past, a fine-grained texture was produced; at others, growth and town design were on a much larger scale. Thus, we find, fossilized in the town's texture, much of the history of its development. To make matters more complicated, we find that, particularly since about 1960, the central (oldest) districts of towns have been renewed, and an ancient medieval urban texture has been destroyed and replaced by one which is better suited to the needs of the motor car. Many ancient towns have lost a great deal of their character in this way. It is important that, as citizens, we must accept that changes are needed to allow us to use motor cars in comparative comfort, but we must take care that the town does not lose its most valuable characteristics in the process. Otherwise we might suddenly realize that we have exchanged the town's heritage for an efficient system of dual carriageways flanked by a monotonous succession of plastic and glass fronted, characterless buildings.

A TYPES OF URBAN TEXTURE

Each stage in the growth of a town has tended to contribute an area with a characteristic texture.

a) The medieval town

In medieval times, towns were mainly used by pedestrians, so many of them had a great number of narrow, winding streets, flanked almost continuously by buildings (fig. 11A). But there were also considerable areas of open space to the rear of the houses, these being reached from the street by means of narrow alleys. In fact, most houses in medieval times had an area of garden, which later often became built-up as the population increased. If the town had been founded by the Romans, like Winchester or Gloucester, or if it had been set up as a fortified bastide (see p.10), like the castle towns of North Wales, it would have a rectangular street plan, often with major streets leading to gates in the town walls. The four main streets of central Gloucester, for example, are named Northgate Street, Southgate Street, Eastgate Street and Westgate Street.

In modern times, the old medieval city is now the city centre and its character has changed enormously. Older property, often of historical importance, has been cleared to make way for shopping centres, office blocks and hotels. The old medieval street pattern has often been regarded as inadequate for motor traffic, so streets have been widened, and pedestrians-only precincts and multi-storey car parks have been built. In some cases much of the medieval street plan has been preserved and new buildings have been erected within this pattern. In the business district of the City of London, for example, high-rise office blocks, competing strongly in altitude with St. Paul's Cathedral, are often reached from narrow streets which have survived since medieval times.

b) The town of the fifteenth to eighteenth centuries

During this time there was a general increase in wheeled traffic in the form of horse-drawn carriages. The growing town was adapted to this development by the provision of wider and straighter streets in the area beyond the limit of the medieval town. In some towns a sudden change in the width of a street can be seen at the point where it crosses the line of the town walls. In this period, well-to-do people still lived near the town centre, and their homes were sometimes built around a garden square which all their families could use (fig. 11B). Many such squares can be seen in London, though their attractions have been diminished by noisy traffic and parked cars.

c) The nineteenth century town

When urban populations began to grow really quickly, in the nineteenth century, builders often aimed to pack as many houses as possible into the smallest possible area. This was often achieved by building houses in long, monotonous rows on each side of streets laid out in a gridiron fashion (fig. 11C). Each house had only a narrow street frontage, so as to reduce road-building costs in relation to the number of houses. Large areas of such housing can be seen in any major British city. The texture is fine-grained within a general gridiron street plan. Occasionally however, larger buildings such as churches, schools and factories occur, embedded in the mass of closely packed houses. Hardly any open spaces exist. Most houses only have a small backyard.

Also, at this time, quite large industrial areas came into existence. Here large, oddly shaped buildings, set at varying angles in relation to one another, are surrounded by yards opening on to streets, and often containing railway sidings. Terraced housing fills any intervening spaces (fig. 11D).

Much 'urban renewal' has taken place in this part of the town. Much of the terraced housing, if regarded as unsuitable for modernization, has been cleared and replaced by inner ring roads, industrial estates and high-rise blocks of residential flats. Since about 1970 there has been a tendency to construct small rows of two, three or four houses, each with a garden area, at quite a low density, instead of high-rise flats.

d) The twentieth century town

At the beginning of the twentieth century it was possible to recognize all the above types of urban texture in large British towns. Twentieth century development has created areas of low density building on the outskirts. Large estates of semi-detached houses and bungalows have been laid out, sometimes with a gridiron street plan and sometimes with curving avenues and many cul-de-sacs (fig. 11E). Houses are much further apart then ever before, and almost every house has a garden larger in area than the house itself. Because of the large building

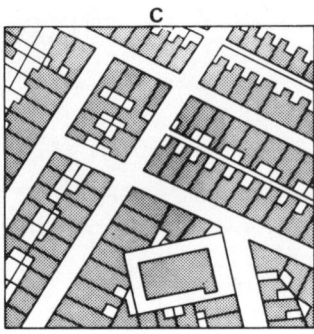

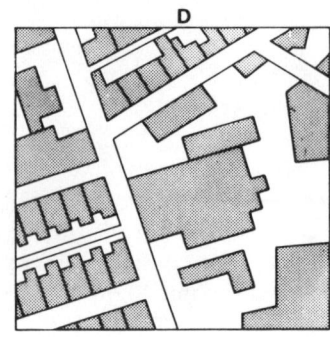

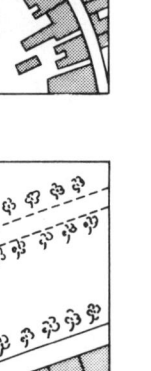

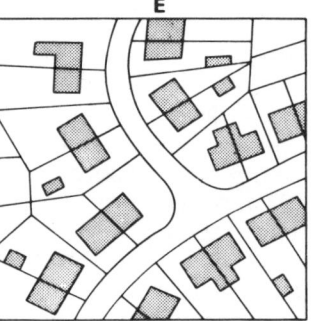

A Medieval town

B Georgian square

C Nineteenth century terraced housing

D Nineteenth century industrial area

E Twentieth century semi-detached housing

figure 11 Urban texture

plots and consequently the very low number of houses per unit area, there are very few roads, quite widely spaced apart. The urban texture is extremely 'loose'. In these residential estates are often single-storey schools and hospitals, surrounded by extensive playing fields and gardens.

Thus, in a British town or city, we would expect to observe a number of contrasting types of urban texture, according to the stages of its growth. In general, the density of both buildings and roads and streets decreases from the centre to the outskirts. The overall road pattern is usually based upon a few major through routes which lead from the centre to the outskirts and onwards to other towns, together with outer ring roads near the periphery and inner ring roads skirting the town centre. Intervening parts of the town are served by a system of 'local access' roads and streets which allow vehicles to reach individual buildings such as houses and factories.

B THE TEXTURE OF CAERNARVON

Figure 12 illustrates the texture of Caernarvon in terms of both buildings and streets. North of the castle is the old walled town or bastide (Area 1), laid out with a rectangular street plan and containing closely packed buildings in a variety of sizes and shapes, with very little open space. From here, this part of the town has grown towards the east and southeast. The areas labelled 2 consist of closely packed rows of terraced housing, with occasional chapels and schools, aligned along a

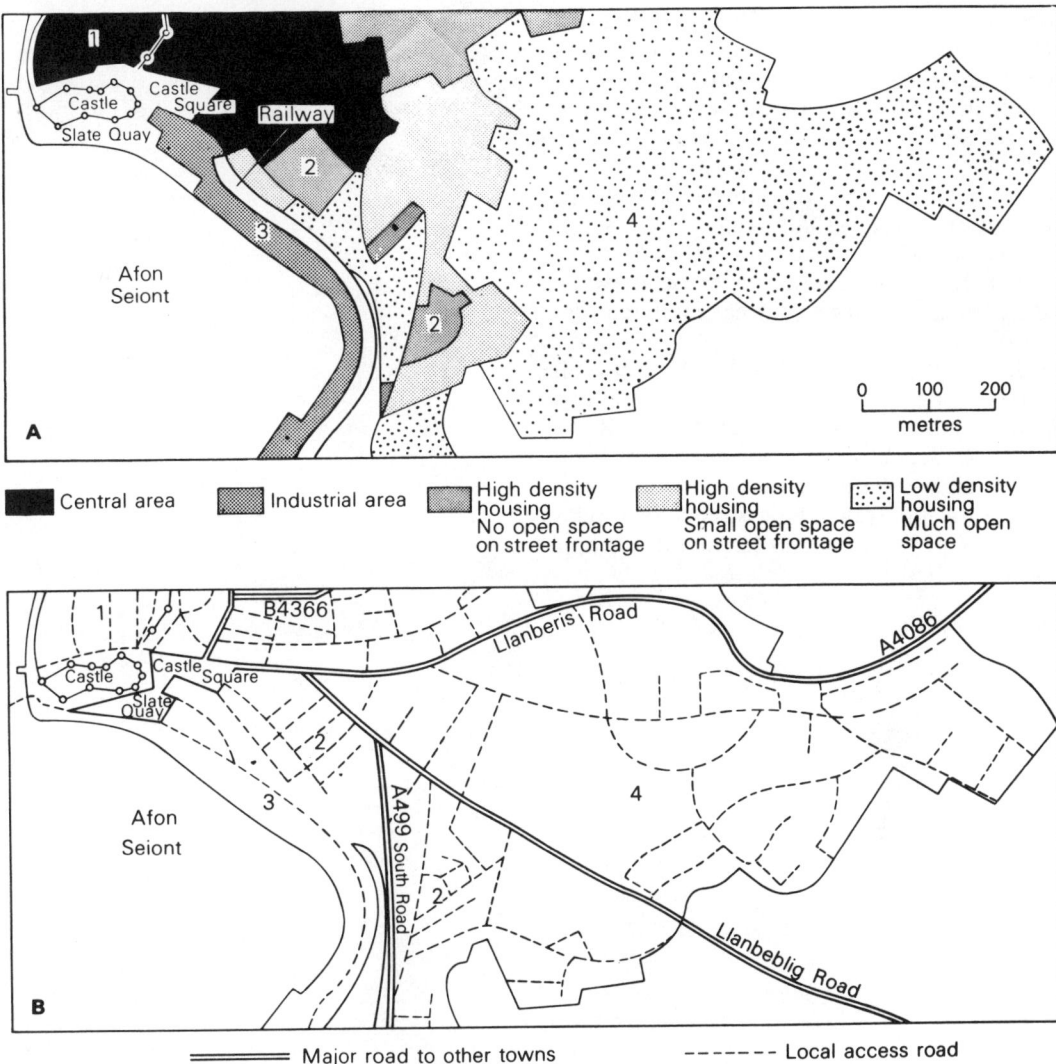

figure 12 The texture of Caernarvon

25

gridiron pattern of streets. These houses front directly on the street; other houses of the high density areas have tiny front gardens. An area of industrial buildings (Area 3) runs between the railway and the river (Afon Seiont). Area 4 is an example of twentieth century development, consisting almost entirely of modern houses, usually in pairs (semi-detached) and provided with large areas of garden. Here, the low density street network forms sweeping curves and has many cul-de-sacs (fig. 12B).

The street plan of this part of Caernarvon is based upon three through routes, Llanberis Road, Llanbeblig Road and South Road (fig. 12B). Between these, a network of local access roads extends as far as the boundary of the built-up area. These streets have relatively few points of access to the three major roads.

Besides existing physically in various shapes and patterns, buildings, roads and open spaces in towns also have functions or uses. By far the greatest part of the space available in a town is devoted to the function of residence. Large areas are also used by shops, offices, industry, parks, schools and hospitals. In many different towns, these functions appear to form very similar patterns, so it seems that some kind of geographical principle influences their distributions.

A A SIMPLE CONCENTRIC MODEL

The best way to understand the patterns of urban functions is to simplify reality by using a model in the first place. Let us imagine a town which is perfectly circular in shape and in which movement is equally easy in all directions. We are assuming that there are no major roads or railways along which movement is particularly easy. Such a town is illustrated in figure 15A on p. 32. Of course, no actual town will be exactly like this. It is fairly obvious that the most accessible place in this imaginary town is the town centre. From all parts of the town, taken as a whole, it is quicker and easier to travel to the town centre than to any other point in the town.

Many different urban functions place a high value on accessibility, because, if they locate themselves in accessible positions, they will make savings in their transport costs. Hence, many different functions will wish to locate in or near the town centre. Of course, they cannot all locate in the most accessible place because there is too little space there, so they compete for this valuable accessible space by offering a price. Like anything else which people want, and which is in short supply, accessible land comes to have a high value. Urban functions bid against one another for accessible locations, which are sold, in general, to the functions which offer the highest prices. Other functions, unable to pay these prices, have to accept less accessible locations in the town. In our simple model, we shall consider only three urban functions: the retail trade (shops), industry (including warehousing or storage) and residence. Other urban functions will be considered in the chapters which follow. How shall we expect these three functions to arrange themselves in the town?

a) Shops

A high level of accessibility is essential for shops because they can only sell their goods if people travel to buy them. Shops therefore need to locate as near as possible to as many customers as possible. Hence, shopkeeping firms will offer high prices for locations in the town centre. A typical 'bid-price curve' for shops is illustrated in the graph in figure 13A. This shows that shops will offer a high 'bid-price' (OA) for locations at the town centre. Away from the town centre, to the right and left on the graph, their bid-price rapidly decreases, until they are not willing to bid at all at any distance greater than OX. Hence, shops will only be willing to bid for space in an area of radius OX surrounding the town centre. Half of this area (a semicircle) is shown in figure 13A.

b) Industry

Industry, on the other hand, may prefer a central, accessible location, but it does not need it to as great an extent as shops. So industry will only bid OB for space in the town centre (see the graph in fig. 13B). Industry, however, while placing a lower value on a central location, will continue to bid for land up to a radius of OY from the town centre (fig. 13B). Thus, industry will bid for space in a much larger area of the town than shops will.

c) Residence

Accessibility is even less important for residence. Some residents may prefer to live fairly near the town centre in order to reduce their travel costs to work, but others will be quite willing to live in inaccessible locations near the edge of the town. The function of residence will tend only to make a low bid (OC) (fig. 13C) for a central position, but it will continue to bid up to a distance of OZ from the town centre. Thus, it is possible for a very large part of the town to be used for residence (see fig. 13C).

d) Competition for urban land

Suppose now that these three functions compete for the available space in the town. We therefore draw all three bid-price curves on the same graph (fig. 13D). On this graph it is now easy to see which function bids the highest for land. Near the town centre, shops outbid the other functions; a little further out industry offers the highest bids. Near the outer edge of the town, shops are no longer bidding, but residence outbids industry. Thus, the map in figure 13D shows concentric rings of shops, industry and residence, arranged around the town centre, each piece of land having gone to the highest bidder. A pattern similar to this is common in European and North American towns. Town centres are dominated by shops, and there is usually a ring of industry, including warehousing, surrounding the town centre. Outer areas tend to be predominantly residential.

e) Urban land values

The value of land in a town is the highest price which any function will pay to occupy and use it. In the graph in figure 13D, the line

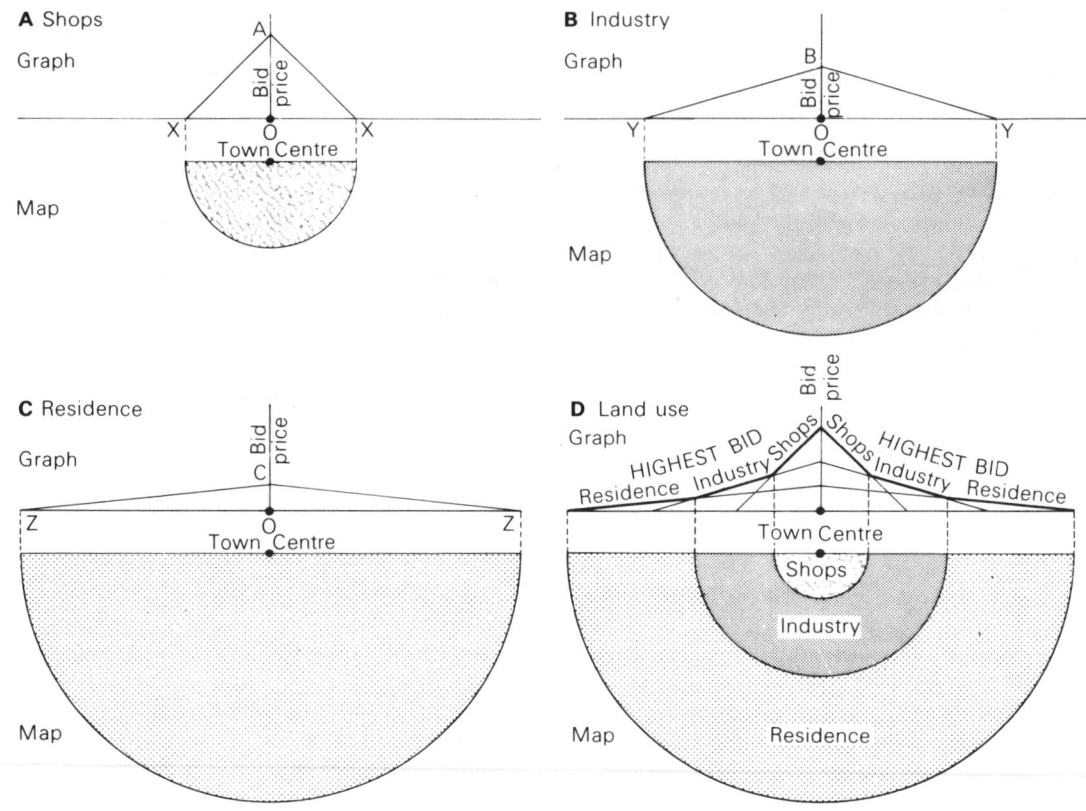

figure 13 Urban land-use patterns: a simple concentric model

labelled 'Highest Bid' shows how the value of land decreases from the centre towards the outskirts. If we were to draw a 'contour' map of land values in this imaginary town, it would show land value isopleths as concentric circles rising to a 'mountain' of high land values in the centre of the town.

B   THE SIMULATION OF A CONCENTRIC PATTERN OF URBAN LAND USE

It will become easier to understand this concentric model of urban land-use if we carry out a simulation exercise rather like the one for urban growth which is explained in Chapter Three. In this simulation we shall create a pattern of land uses on a set of 59 hexagonal cells (fig. 14) representing a complete town. We shall allow shops, industry and residence to bid for each cell in turn.

a)   The weighting process

Each cell is weighted according to the principles outlined earlier in this chapter. High weights are given to cells which the particular function values highly.
1   In the case of shops (fig. 14A), the central cell is given a weight of 12, the ring of six cells surrounding it 8, and the ring of twelve cells surrounding these, 4. All other cells carry a weight of 0, indicating that shops are unwilling to bid for these locations.
2   In industry (fig. 14B), the central cell is weighted at 8, and successive rings working outwards at 6, 4, 2 and 1 respectively. The four corner cells are weighted at 0.

3   The central cell in the case of residence is given a weight of 6 (fig. 14C). Then weights are reduced outwards from the centre to 5, 4, 3 and 2. The four corner cells have a weight of 1, so it is clear that these cells can only be allocated to residence.

b)   The bidding process

Bids are made by each function for each cell in turn, beginning in the north-west corner and working either from north to south or from west to east.

As in the urban growth simulation, we introduce a 'chance' factor to represent the element of uncertainty in the buying, selling or leasing of land. A bid is therefore made by using the random sampling numbers listed in Table III. In this table, the digits are arranged in groups of three, in each of which the first digit is used for the bid from shops, the second for the bid from industry, and the third for the bid from residence, for any single cell. The actual value of a bid by any function is its random digit multiplied by its weight for the particular cell.

Suppose, for example, we are conducting the bidding for the cell labelled X in figure 14A, B, C and D, and the group of random digits is 642. The bid for the cell from shops will be 6 (random digit) × 0 (weight for cell) = 0, so the bid of 0 is recorded in this cell in figure 14A. Similarly the bid from industry is 4 (random digit) × 2 (weight) = 8, and this bid is recorded in figure 14B. The bid from residence (2 × 3 = 6) is recorded in cell X in figure 14C. The higest bid for this cell is therefore 8, from industry, so the bid of 8 in figure 14B is ringed to indicate that this cell

has been allocated to industry. The cell can now be shaded in figure 14D in the style used for industry. This process is carried out for every cell in the town.

If there is a tie between two functions in the bidding, the bidding is repeated using the next group of three random digits, but only the tied functions may rebid, the remaining digit being ignored. The final recorded bid for the particular cell is the largest bid offered by the function in both rounds of bidding. In the cell marked Y, for example (fig. 14A, B and C), both shops and industry bid 28 in the first round, with residence bidding only 12. In the rebid, shops bid 20 and industry only 4. The cell is therefore allocated to shops at a bid of 28, and a bid of 28 is also recorded for industry.

c)   Analysis of the land-use pattern

The final land-use pattern is illustrated in figure 14D. It is not possible, of course, to see at a glance to what extent a concentric pattern exists. We therefore divide the town into four concentric zones (fig. 14E). The results of the analysis in terms of these four zones are tabulated in Table IV.

We are also able to construct a map showing land values in the town (fig. 14F). This is done by recording the 'winning' bid at the centre of each cell, and then drawing isopleths.

A   Weights and bids for shops

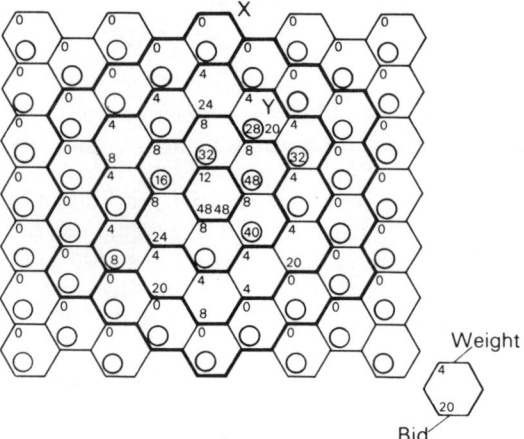

B   Weights and bids for industry

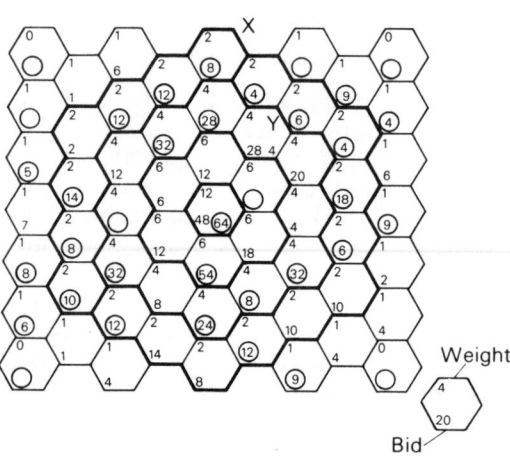

C   Weights and bids for residence

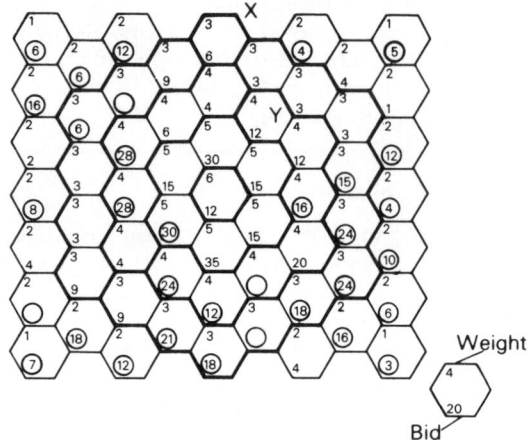

D   Land use map

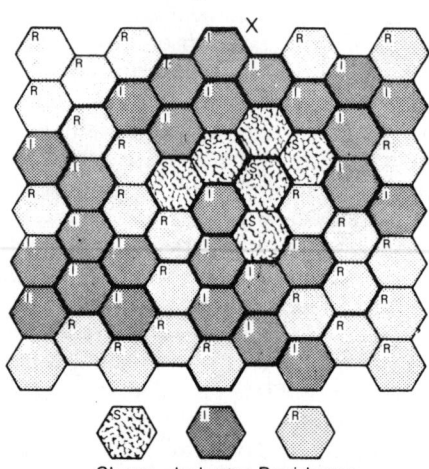

Shops   Industry   Residence

E   Concentric zones for use in analysis

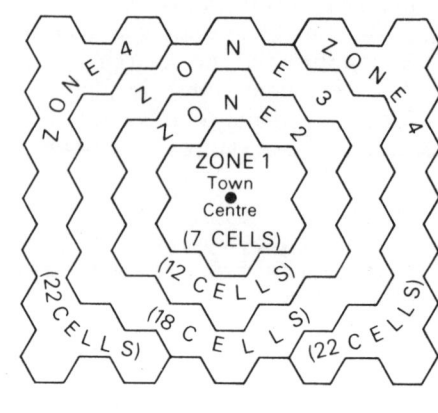

F   Land values

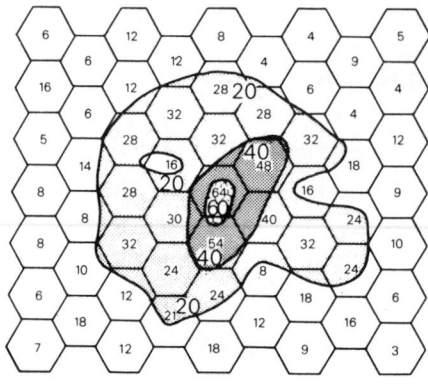

figure 14 Simulation of a simple concentric pattern of urban land uses

TABLE III   *Random sampling numbers for simulation of urban land-use*

707	228	078	917	443	284	120	246	362	585	773	920	126	087	756
835	978	059	455	063	805	425	608	562	956	471	225	552	767	071
439	495	584	767	002	475	094	851	377	892	912	105	425	930	680
290	684	236	329	539	166	581	274	324	592	268	290	636	863	128
840	096	919	498	654	035	933	382	617	821	098	274	826	189	518
479	417	014	313	915	683	053	560	462	295	578	073	691	719	103
133	105	765	218	378	348	736	167	426	738	112	294	053	600	146
662	387	863	610	734	209	275	813	408	358	277	662	106	966	385
743	581	173	044	418	208	688	912	079	048	334	217	883	751	000
197	914	369	504	116	530	329	771	236	475	024	686	864	461	101
770	779	531	909	405	836	532	541	764	841	819	733	008	382	159
071	331	559	721	811	665	634	453	812	666	101	788	488	367	205
833	794	339	793	155	489	517	119	737	892	052	868	262	275	284
741	587	268	488	865	845	976	566	571	425	326	159	292	549	966
128	027	211	136	971	064	409	460	630	743	801	601	886	904	360
596	748	660	942	537	310	779	237	533	303	240	984	669	570	993
985	322	413	071	745	196	458	007	102	631	108	234	446	025	613
948	296	227	529	352	439	342	281	800	084	036	125	608	528	716
576	771	248	669	919	556	356	663	006	937	333	303	733	688	536
530	797	868	935	979	606	154	846	620	837	955	681	105	960	512
571	148	054	857	263	411	979	563	613	209	949	594	548	038	375
909	903	395	738	712	714	041	086	835	242	185	754	947	052	280
088	903	957	634	219	658	695	213	041	867	790	866	961	572	454

TABLE IV   *Analysis of the land-use pattern*

A   Number of cells occupied by each function

	Shops	Industry	Residence	Total
Zone 1	4	2	1	7
Zone 2	2	6	4	12
Zone 3	0	12	6	18
Zone 4	0	7	15	22

B   Percentage of area occupied by each function

	Shops	Industry	Residence	Total
Zone 1	57	29	14	100
Zone 2	17	50	33	100
Zone 3	0	67	33	100
Zone 4	0	32	68	100

C   Average bid per cell

	Shops	Industry	Residence
Zone 1	30	24	22
Zone 2	13	19	14
Zone 3	0	9	10
Zone 4	0	4	7

D   Average land value

Zone 1	41
Zone 2	26
Zone 3	13
Zone 4	9

Table IVA and B indicates that shops dominate the central part of the town (Zone 1), industry dominates Zones 2 and 3, and residence Zone 4, as we would expect. Table IVC shows that the average bids of each function decrease with distance from the town centre, shops most steeply and residence most gradually. As expected, Table IVD shows a steady decrease in average land values from the town centre to the outskirts.

The land value map (fig. 14F) shows a fairly clear concentric pattern rising to a peak in the centre of the town. Only three low-value cells (sold at 16, 16 and 8 respectively) interfere with the generally circular pattern of the isopleths.

C MORE COMPLEX MODELS

In the simple model explained above, it was assumed that movement was equally easy in all parts of the town and that accessibility increased to a maximum at the town centre. We shall now approach a little nearer to the much more complex conditions existing in an actual town.

a) A Radial-concentric model

1 In the simple model we have assumed that accessibility decreases at an even rate outwards from the town centre. This clearly is not the case in reality. We have already seen (page 13) that British towns often have a pattern of main roads radiating from the town centre. These roads are channels of easy movement so they provide radial zones of high accessibility. Hence, various land uses will bid a higher price for locations along these roads than for the areas which lie between them. We would therefore expect shops, which place a high value on accessibility, to extend along these radial roads from the town centre. Most roads leading to the centres of British towns do of course illustrate

this tendency quite clearly. Similarly, we might expect other land uses to 'push' outwards along the roads, as shown in figure 15B. Because land uses are bidding highly for these roadside locations, 'spurs' of high land values will extend along the radial roads from the 'peak' in the town centre.

Accessibility has also been improved in a vertical sense by the invention of the lift. The most accessible part of a building in a town centre is the ground floor, that people can simply walk into. To reach the upper floors it is often necessary to climb stairs. The installation of lifts and escalators in town centre shops has made the higher floors of buildings very nearly as accessible as the ground floors. Hence, the shopping function has tended to extend upwards. It is common nowadays to find five or six floors in town centre buildings devoted to the shopping function. Where no lift exists, shopping is usually restricted to one or two floors only.

Other urban features may contribute to this radial pattern of urban functions. Often a river, a canal or a railway runs from the centre of the town towards its outskirts. Industry particularly has been attracted to these zones. A simplified radial-concentric pattern of land uses is illustrated in figure 15B.

2 Figure 16 shows the results of a simulation exercise carried out for a town which has three main roads radiating from its centre. Shops, in particular, have gained roadside sites, even at some distance from the town centre, whereas residence tends to occupy the spaces between the roads.

The map of land values (fig. 16B) illustrates both the concentric and radial patterns. In general, land values rise to a central 'peak'

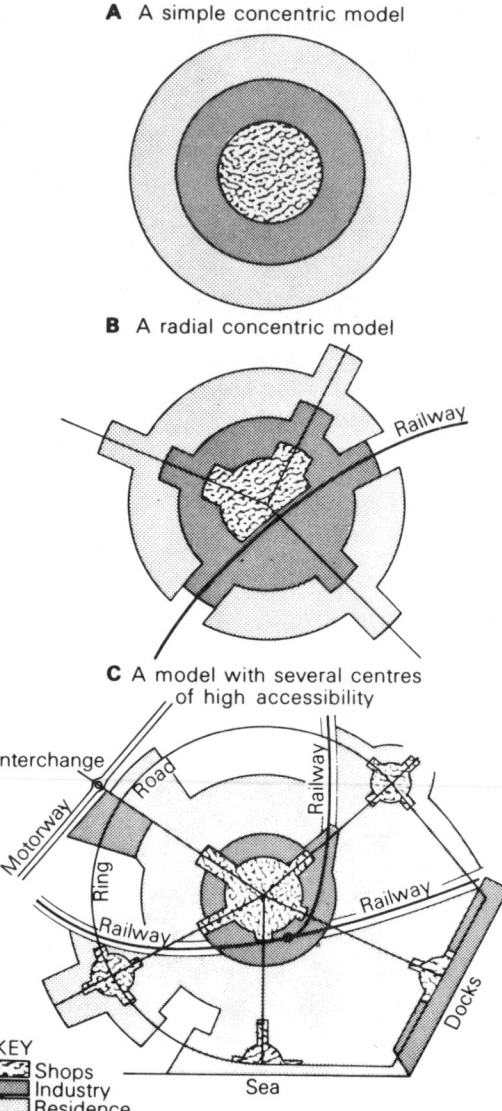

A A simple concentric model

B A radial concentric model

C A model with several centres of high accessibility

KEY
Shops
Industry
Residence

A Land use map

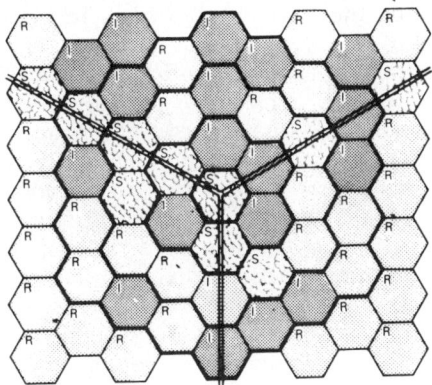

B Land values

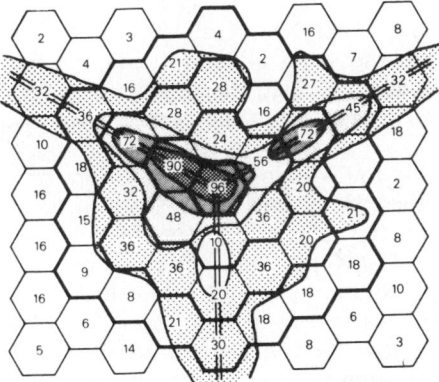

figure 16 Simulation of a radial-concentric pattern of urban land use

figure 15 Urban land-use patterns

and the isopleth for a value of 20 is roughly circular in the spaces between the roads. The higher land values, however, are strikingly elongated along two of the roads.

b) A Model with several centres of high accessibility

1 So far we have tended to assume that a high degree of accessibility only exists at the town centre and along the radial roads near it. In modern times, with the growing use of cars for personal transport, traffic congestion and difficulties of parking have tended to reduce accessibility in the town centre. Cars and lorries are not restricted to movement along bus routes; they are able to move fairly freely through the town's road and street network, so accessibility has improved in many different parts of the town.

Points of very high accessibility are found at junctions of radial roads and ring roads, and shops are often attracted to these locations (fig. 15c). Supermarkets, which need large areas of parking space, are often found here, and sometimes large integrated shopping centres. In Britain there would be many more large shopping centres and hypermarkets on the outskirts of our towns, but for planning restrictions. Other highly accessible locations exist where there is a motorway interchange on the outskirts of a town. Here again is a valuable site for large shops or an industrial estate (fig. 15c). The motorway gives access to a much larger area than the single town. Similarly, in a seaside town, industry tends to locate near the docks, which of course provide accessibility to the rest of the world. The function of residence

will bid highly to occupy urban space with pleasant views, especially of the sea in a seaside town, but residence will tend to avoid areas where noisy, dirty or smelly industries affect the environment.

Thus, we would expect particular land uses to be attracted to many different parts of the town, not only to the town centre. Isolated 'peaks', 'ridges' or 'plateaux' of high land values will be found in these areas.

2 In figure 17 are illustrated the land use and land values maps produced by a simulation exercise relating to this kind of pattern of urban functions. The town has a network of major roads, with four important junctions in addition to the town centre. In the southeast is an area of docks, and in the south-west an area with pleasant views of the sea.

Shops and industry bids have been weighted highly in road cells which have road junctions, and also fairly highly along the roads. Also, industry has been given a high weighting near the docks. The cells with a sea view have been weighted highly for residence.

Shops and industry dominate the roadside locations (fig. 17a). Shops are clustered strongly near the town centre, occupying five of the seven central cells, and also extend outwards along the roads. Industry is mainly concentrated in the east of the town, chiefly in the area immediately surrounding the central shopping district and near the docks. Residence, on the other hand is mainly in the western part of the town, usually occupying the spaces between the main roads, except in the area with the sea view.

Land values rise to a high level (96) in the town centre (fig. 17b), and other areas with values of over 60 are found in the south-west

A Land use map

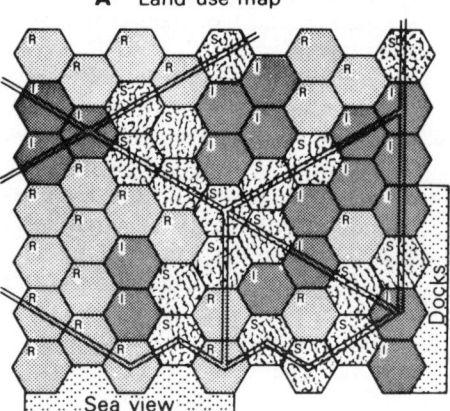

B Land values

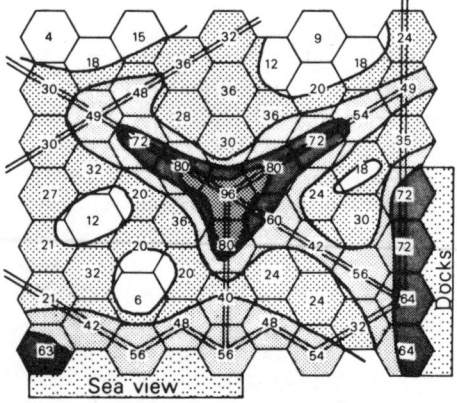

figure 17 Simulation of a pattern of urban land use with several centres of high accessibility

(sea view) and south-east (docks). Corridors of relatively high land values extend along the major roads. It is clear that three major centres of high land values exist. Patches of low land values clearly occupy the spaces between the major roads.

D THE LAND-USE PATTERN OF VANCOUVER

Vancouver, the largest city in British Columbia in Canada, is situated on a peninsula between a distributary of the Fraser river in the south and Burrard Inlet in the north (fig. 18). Recent urban growth has extended the urbanized area eastwards, northwards across Burrard Inlet, and southwards across the Fraser. The area shown in figure 18 is the City of Vancouver, as distinct from Greater Vancouver.

On the 'downtown peninsula', between False Creek and Burrard Inlet, is located Vancouver's central shopping district, fringed on three sides by industrial areas (fig. 18A). Industry, attracted by the harbour facilities, occupies most of the south shore of Burrard Inlet and also the banks of the North Arm of the Fraser river where there are many timber processing plants. The railway yards at the east end of False Creek also appear to have attracted a concentration of industry. Wholesale traders are particularly important in the downtown peninsula and in the False Creek area.

Shops and other commercial enterprises such as restaurants, motels, hotels and 'auto rows' (car sales establishments) are clearly orientated to the rectangular street pattern of the city, running generally in long, narrow strips along these streets (fig. 18A). In most of Vancouver, except for the far north-east, 'streets' run from north to south and 'avenues' from east to west. 'Streets' are generally given names, such as Granville Street and Cambie Street, but 'avenues' are numbered, from First Avenue near False Creek to Seventy-seventh Avenue near the Fraser river. Kingsway, an important commercial strip, runs at an angle, cutting across the rectangular network. Oakridge, where Forty-first Avenue crosses Cambie Street ('41st and Cambie'), is a recently developed regional shopping centre, where shops form a compact group and parking facilities are provided.

Specimen land values, for both commercial and industrial land, are shown in figure 18B, C and D. Two features are clear. In general, commercial land has a higher value than industrial land. Also, all land values, whether commercial or industrial, appear in general to decrease away from the central shopping area.

It is easy to distinguish the most important part of the central business district in figure 18B, where the value of commercial land rises well over $80.00 per square foot. In much of this area, commercial land values have risen by over 200 per cent in two years (fig. 18C). Moving outwards from the commercial centre of the city, land values decrease, but they still remain quite high on Granville Street and Broadway. Figure 18C shows that the rate of increase in the value of commercial land decreases with distance from the central business district.

The highest industrial land values are found along the banks of False Creek, comparatively near the central business district (fig. 18D). They fall much lower in the east of the city and along the Fraser river in the south, relatively remote from the downtown peninsula.

Vancouver appears to be a particularly good illustration of our model in which there are several centres of high accessibility (page 33).

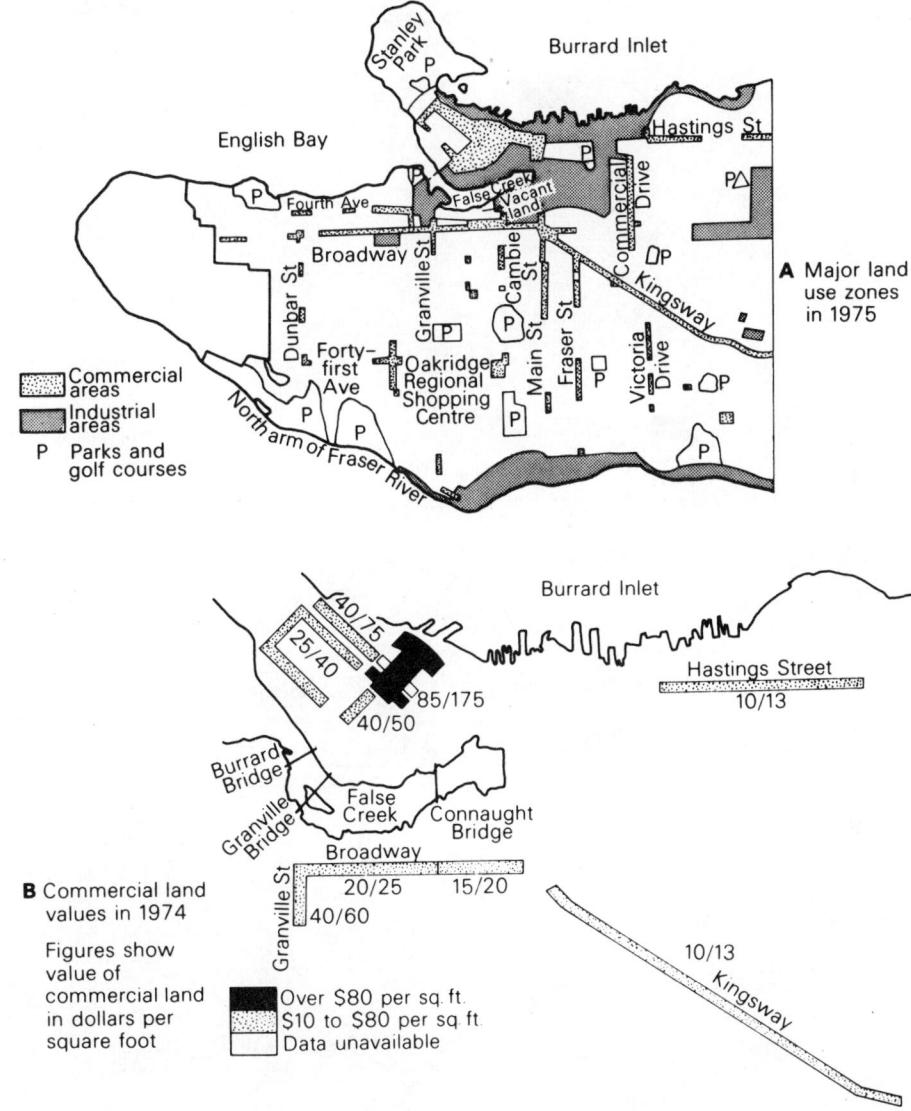

A Major land use zones in 1975

Commercial areas
Industrial areas
P Parks and golf courses

B Commercial land values in 1974

Figures show value of commercial land in dollars per square foot

Over $80 per sq. ft.
$10 to $80 per sq. ft.
Data unavailable

figure 18 General pattern of urban land use in Vancouver

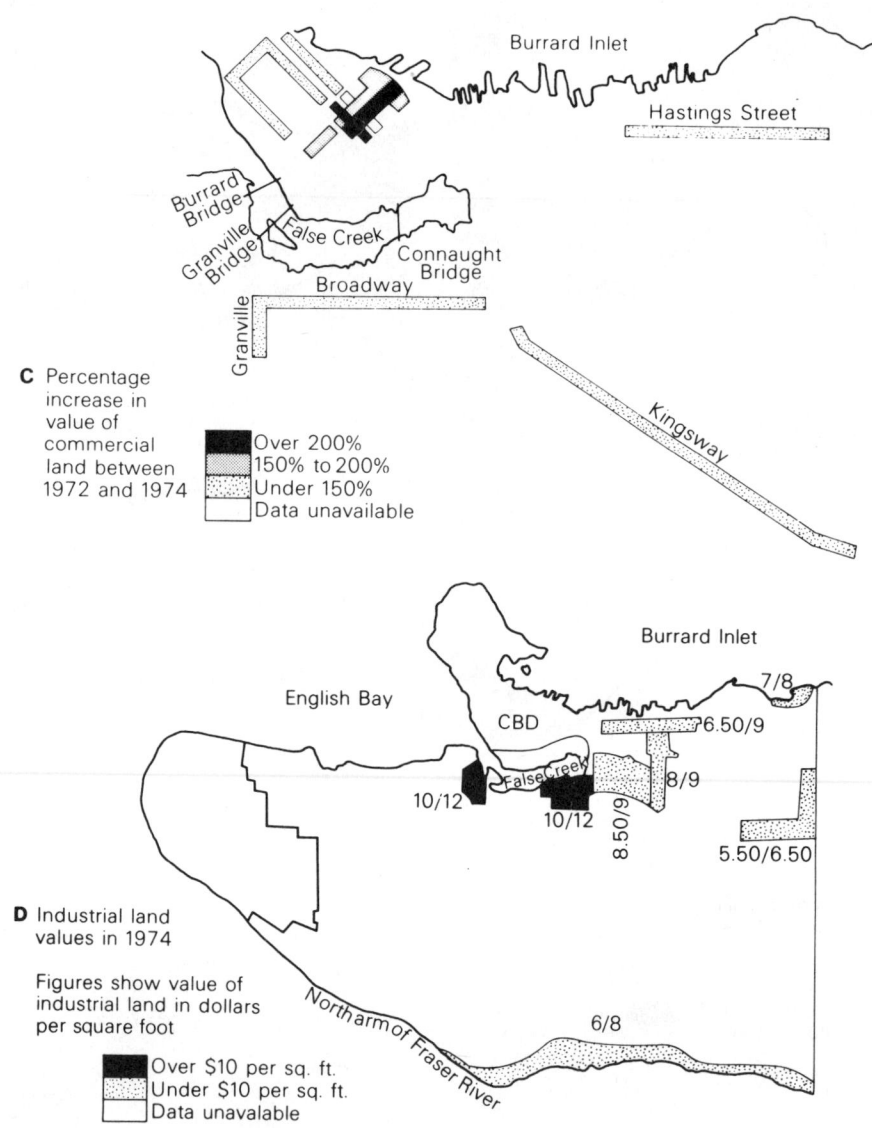

Burrard Inlet

Hastings Street

Burrard Bridge

Granville Bridge

False Creek

Connaught Bridge

Broadway

Granville

Kingsway

C Percentage increase in value of commercial land between 1972 and 1974

Over 200%
150% to 200%
Under 150%
Data unavailable

Burrard Inlet

English Bay

CBD

False Creek

7/8

6.50/9

8/9

10/12

10/12

8.50/9

5.50/6.50

D Industrial land values in 1974

Figures show value of industrial land in dollars per square foot

Over $10 per sq. ft.
Under $10 per sq. ft.
Data unavalable

North arm of Fraser River

6/8

We have seen in Chapter Five that shops place a high value on accessibility to their customers, and therefore tend to cluster in the town centre itself, along the radial roads leading from it, and at important road junctions in other parts of the town. Let us now study the distribution of shop types in more detail. In the late nineteenth century, shops progressively replaced residences in the centres of British towns, to such an extent that these areas have come to be known as 'central business districts'. Other groups of shops in other parts of the town are referred to as 'suburban shopping centres'. In general, one would expect between 8% and 15% of a town's shops to be located in its central business district.

A CONVENIENCE GOODS AND SHOPPING GOODS

We can only understand the pattern of shops in a town by reference to the types of goods or services which they sell to the public. It is useful therefore to make a distinction between convenience goods (and services) and shopping goods (and services).

Convenience goods are those which people buy frequently and on which comparatively little is spent on a single shopping trip. They include foods such as groceries, greengroceries, meat, sweets and tobacco, and services such as ladies' hairdressing. These kinds of goods and services are bought regularly by practically every household in the town, so it is an advantage to the customers if the shops which supply them are scattered widely through the town. Such shops can usually be operated quite successfully as small units, so they tend to be distributed in such a way that their customers have only to travel very short distances to reach them (fig. 19A).

figure 19 Convenience goods and shopping goods

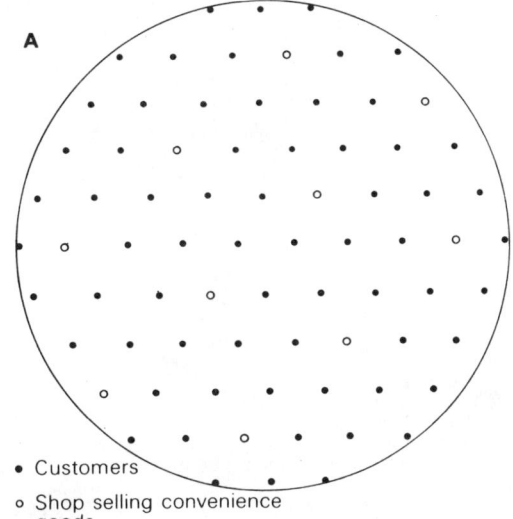

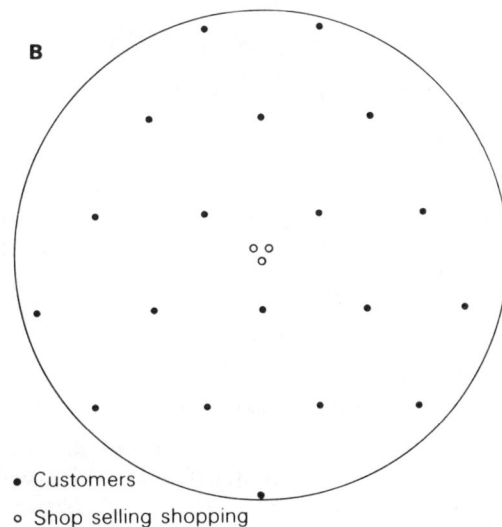

Shopping goods, on the other hand, are bought much less frequently, and often a large sum of money is spent during a single shopping trip. Typical shopping goods include clothing, shoes, furniture, electrical goods and jewellery. In any particular week it is likely that only a small proportion of the townspeople will buy these goods. Buyers therefore are likely to be thinly and probably fairly evenly distributed through the town (fig. 19B). Shops selling these goods usually have to be quite large, so as to carry sufficient stocks to provide their customers with a choice. Also, when buyers are making such purchases, they will tend to want to 'shop around' and make comparisons of prices, styles and quality between a number of shops. Because purchases are relatively infrequent, buyers will be prepared to make a longer journey than they would to buy simple food necessities. Hence, it is an advantage for such shops to cluster in the centre of the town or in large suburban shopping centres.

In many British towns there are at least 50% more shops selling convenience goods than shopping goods. In their central business districts however, there are two or three times more shops selling shopping goods than convenience goods. Clothing, shoe and furniture shops and large variety and department stores are strongly concentrated in central business districts.

B A HIERARCHY OF SHOPPING CENTRES

We would therefore expect a town to possess a hierarchy of shopping centres, ranging from the central business district down to the small corner shop. Figure 20 gives a generalized picture of the distribution of such a hierarchy in an imaginary town.

a) The Central business district

This is the largest concentration of shops in the town, up to three-quarters of which will be selling shopping goods. It is centrally located within the town, and the market area from which it draws its customers extends over the entire town and even beyond, to other smaller towns and villages. About 30% to 35% of the shops sell clothing or shoes, and about 20% sell household goods including furniture. Generally, under 20% of its shops are concerned with the sale of food, though its market may contain many food stalls.

b) Suburban shopping centres

These shop groups are often located in positions of high accessibility in other parts of the town, perhaps along major roads or at road junctions. They contain a higher proportion of shops selling convenience goods than the central business district, but some of them may still have a considerable number of shopping-goods shops. It seems likely that the proportion of shopping-goods will be greater in larger shopping centres than in smaller ones, but we shall investigate this a little later. Suburban shopping centres vary greatly in size, from groups of well over a hundred shops down to the single corner shop, often a grocery or off-licence.

C THE COMPOSITION OF SUBURBAN SHOPPING CENTRES

It is suggested above that the proportion of shopping-goods shops will be greater in large shopping centres than in small ones. It will be interesting to find out whether this is so in an actual example. We shall use a sample of shopping centres in Blackpool, which was surveyed in 1970. In this exercise we are regarding convenience-goods shops as comprising food shops, confectioners and newsagents, together with a variety of service shops, such as post offices, hairdressers and launderettes. Clothing, shoes, household goods and non-food goods generally are being regarded as shopping goods. All the necessary data relating to thirteen shopping centres are given in Table V.

The first impression is that these shopping centres have a very high proportion of shops dealing in shopping goods. This may be connected with the fact that Blackpool is an

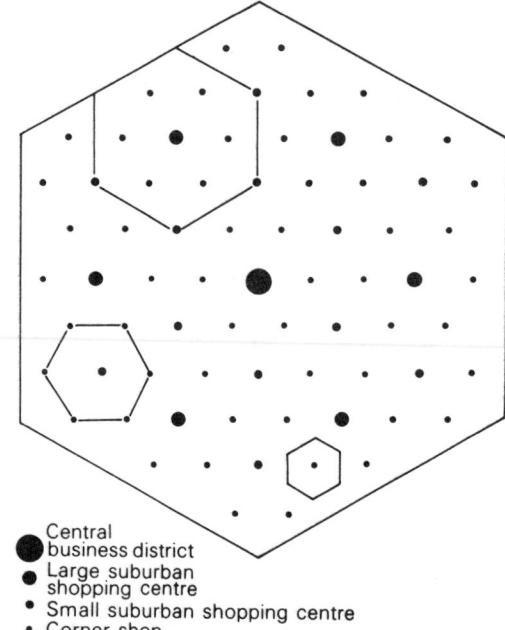

● Central business district
● Large suburban shopping centre
• Small suburban shopping centre
· Corner shop

figure 20

TABLE V   *A sample of shopping centres in Blackpool*

Index Letter of Centre	Number of Shops in Centre		Percentage of Shopping-goods Shops	
	Total	Rank Order	Total	Rank Order
A	184	1	74.5	6
B	183	2	79.8	2
C	182	3	75.3	5
D	109	4	76.1	4
E	102	5	81.4	1
F	90	6	62.2	12
G	81	7	77.8	3
H	65	8	73.8	8
J	42	9	69.0	10
K	39	10	74.4	7
L	31	11.5	71.0	9
M	31	11.5	64.5	11
N	26	13	57.7	13

Note: If two centres have the same number of shops their rank orders are the average of the two ranks they occupy. Centres L and M occupy ranks 11 and 12, so their rank order is 11.5.

TABLE VI   *Shopping centres of Blackpool: rank correlation*

Index Letter of Centre	Number of Shops Rank Order	Percentage of Shopping-goods Shops Rank Order	D	D^2
A	1	6	5	25
B	2	2	0	0
C	3	5	2	4
D	4	4	0	0
E	5	1	4	16
F	6	12	6	36
G	7	3	4	16
H	8	8	0	0
J	9	10	1	1
K	10	7	3	9
L	11.5	9	2.5	6.25
M	11.5	11	0.5	0.25
N	13	13	0	0
				———
				$\Sigma D^2 = 113.5$

important holiday resort. In Table V the centres have been ranked in order of total shops and also in order of their percentage of shops selling shopping goods. If it is true that shops selling shopping goods are more concentrated in the larger shopping centres, we would expect these two lists of ranks to be very much alike. Even if they are not exactly alike, they may be similar enough for us to be reasonably sure that their resemblance is not just accidental. To discover whether this is so, we need to carry out a simple exercise in correlation.

The two lists of ranks are given in Table VI. In this table the differences between the two ranks for each centre are listed in the column headed D. In the column headed D^2 each of these rank differences is squared and the sum of this column (ΣD^2) is 113.5. Of course, we cannot yet tell whether this figure is small enough to indicate that there is a close correlation between the two lists of ranks. Turning to figure 21, however, and plotting the position of a ΣD^2 value of 113.5 against 13 shopping centres (Point X), we see that a 'significant positive correlation' is indicated. This means that it is unlikely that the similarity between the two ranking lists could have occurred by accident. We are therefore justified in stating that the larger shopping centres of Blackpool tend to have a higher proportion of shopping-goods shops than the smaller centres.

In the city of Vancouver a distinct hierarchy of suburban shopping centres is recognized. In the 'regional' centre, Oakridge (fig. 18), serving a market area of up to 300 000 people, 75 % of the shops sell shopping goods. In the fourteen 'district' centres, each serving

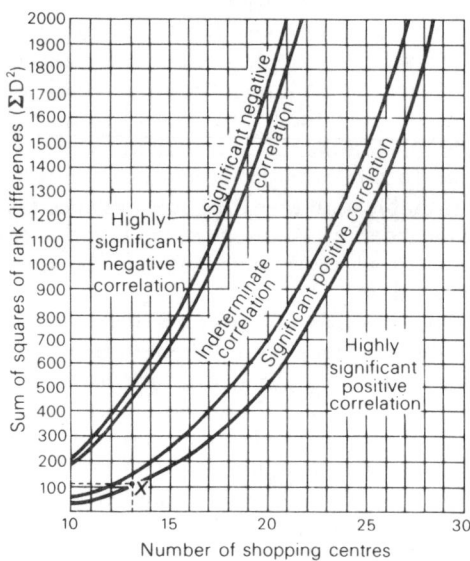

figure 21 Graph to test the significance of rank correlation

a population of up to 50 000, 50% of the shops sell shopping goods. There are 75 'local' centres generally serving market areas of under 10 000, and in these, shopping-goods shops make up about 25% of the total number of shops.

D MODERN DEVELOPMENTS

Important developments have taken place in the retail trade since the Second World War. The level of car ownership has increased and people have become much more willing to travel considerable distances on shopping trips. Improvements in home storage facilities have meant that very frequent shopping for convenience goods has declined. A pattern of weekly shopping trips by car has developed even for food buying. This tendency has been helped by the development of supermarkets, where prices may be reduced through savings made through bulk buying and reductions in labour costs by pre-packing and self-service.

Early supermarkets tended to locate within central business districts, but these were usually small and had inadequate parking facilities. More recently, huge shops (super-stores, hypermarkets, discount warehouses) have developed, often in the outer areas of towns where large car-parking facilities could be provided. This major development has tended to draw trade away from traditional central business districts and also from small local shopping centres.

To some extent, the central business districts have tended to retaliate in the face of this competition, by developing integrated shopping complexes in which a number of different shops occupy a pleasant, heated, and sometimes carpeted, shopping mall, often equipped with escalators. Attempts have been made to overcome the shortage of space by the provision of roof-top or underground parking or multistorey car parks.

E OFFICES

The distribution of offices in towns appears to follow the same general principles as that of shops. But a major difference is that there are far fewer offices of the 'convenience' type than there are shops of this type. It is unusual for people to make regular, frequent journeys to visit an office. The offices of solicitors, estate agents, insurance companies and others are visited only rarely, so it is not surprising to find that they are strongly concentrated in central business districts. Other offices, such as banks, and the surgeries of doctors and dentists may be visited more regularly, so they tend to be scattered more widely through the town in locations which are convenient to relatively small groups of customers.

In general, offices are concentrated in central business districts to a much greater extent than shops. This is partly because their market areas so frequently extend over the whole town, and partly because many offices perform services for other organizations which exist in the town centre. The so-called 'functional linkages' between offices are much stronger than between shops. Accountants, advertizing agents and solicitors, for example, are frequently employed by other firms within the central business district. Local government offices, such as the Labour Exchange, are also almost invariably located centrally, because they serve the whole town. Some office firms may well consider that they need a central location so as to obtain the prestige of an address in a well-known street, in order to inspire confidence in potential customers.

In many large towns, offices provide employment for well over half of the working population of the central business district. The daily ebb and flow of office workers is the cause of much traffic congestion in the central districts of towns.

In Chapter Five we have seen that shops in particular will bid highly for space in the centre of a town. In Chapter Six we have seen that shops selling shopping goods in particular tend to congregate in the central business district where they can gain a high level of accessibility to the town as a whole. We shall now take a closer look at the characteristics of the central business district.

A GENERAL CHARACTERISTICS OF THE CENTRAL BUSINESS DISTRICT

The central business district is usually situated at or near the early nucleus of the town, where the town's major roads converge. In the middle of the nineteenth century this area had many different functions. It was often predominantly residential, but it also contained churches, schools, and a good deal of small-scale industry and commerce. As time went by, the residential function declined, as people moved towards the outer edge of the growing town, and also manufacturing industry migrated outwards. Land in the town centre became too valuable to be used in these ways, and more intensive land uses superseded residence and industry. The central business district developed, dominated by

urban functions which could make the best use of its advantages of accessibility.

The central business district is now characterized by the presence of shops, often very large and specialized, offices, including those of solicitors, accountants, insurance companies, local and national government, cinemas, theatres, hotels and restaurants. Many of these are intended to provide a service for the entire population of the town and sometimes the surrounding areas; others provide services for the workers and shoppers who visit the area daily. As well as the churches, many of the old residential buildings still exist, though they have often been altered almost beyond recognition. New shop fronts have been added to older buildings, but the upper floors and the rears of buildings may sometimes remain almost unchanged. Urban renewal is almost continuous as worn-out buildings are replaced by new.

In general, the size of the central business district increases as the town's population increases, but it may well be that there is a maximum size above which the district cannot continue to function efficiently. Since movement within the central business district is predominantly on foot, it is likely that the friction of distance restricts its expansion in the same way as in the medieval town. There is much competition between different land uses for this limited amount of valuable space.

Hence, it is common for the central business district to expand upwards.

The skyscraper was invented in the late nineteenth century to provide space for urban functions which do not need a location at ground level yet place a high value on a position in the centre of the town. By the use of lifts, the various floors of skyscrapers are more accessible to pedestrians than they would be if they were laid out side by side along the ground (fig. 22). Skyscrapers are not very common in British towns, but town centre buildings are frequently much taller than those in the rest of the town. The multi-storey car park follows the same principle as the skyscraper. If all cars had to be parked on the level, the central business district would be in great danger of growing to a quite unmanageable size for pedestrians. On Manhattan Island in the city of New York, a great

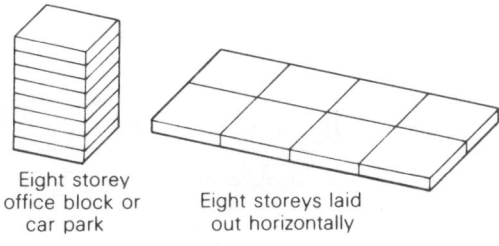

Eight storey office block or car park

Eight storeys laid out horizontally

figure 22 Space-saving by multistorey buildings

deal of vertical expansion has taken place. Here the amount of central space is strictly limited by the surrounding water areas.

Traffic in the central business district is extremely dense, with cars and other vehicles on the roads, and pedestrians on the pavements. Many problems have therefore arisen. When cars are used for journeys to the town centre, valuable space has to be used to store the vehicle until the return journey is made. If unrestricted parking were permitted, the accumulation of parked vehicles would seriously hinder the flow of moving vehicles. Hence, parking is usually restricted, in larger towns often by the use of meters. In fact, the 'meter zone' of a large town may be roughly coincident with the area of the central business district. Problems also arise when a conflict occurs between the flow of vehicles and the flow of pedestrians. Hence, in places, special arrangements are made for pedestrian traffic to cross the path of vehicular traffic by the creation of subways or controlled crossings. Many towns have developed complex arrangements to separate pedestrians completely from vehicles in busy shopping areas, by creating 'pedestrian precincts' from which vehicles are completely excluded. Arrangements are often made for vans to make deliveries to shops at a higher or lower level than that which is restricted to pedestrians (fig. 23).

B PATTERNS OF LAND USE IN THE CENTRAL BUSINESS DISTRICT

a) Accessibility to the pedestrian

Much of the detailed land-use pattern of the central business district may be understood partly in terms of the principle of accessibility to the pedestrian. There is often a close relationship between the pattern of land use and the volume of pedestrian flows.

Shops require this type of accessibility most of all. They have to attract customers before any trade can take place. Hence, they need display space at pavement level. Large stores such as department stores and variety stores need accessibility to pedestrians most of all. These shops can only operate on a very large scale, so it is essential that they succeed in maintaining a high volume of sales. They therefore tend to occupy the frontages of the major shopping streets of the town, sometimes using a complete block and enjoying frontages on four different streets. Pedestrian flows of very high volume occur near these shops. Men's and women's clothing shops and shoe shops also tend to occupy prominent positions along major street frontages where land values are particularly high. Banks often occur in association with these shops. Corner sites are particularly prized because here a number of different pedestrian flows may converge. These functions use space intensively and have a large turnover of money per square foot of sales space. They can therefore afford to bid highly for these advantageous sites. Other shops, such as furniture shops, need a greater amount of display space and may therefore use space less intensively and be relegated to less accessible locations. Eastgate Street, in Gloucester (fig. 25), illustrates the intensive use of highly accessible urban space. Here large stores, banks and national multiple clothing and shoe shops occupy much of the street frontage.

Offices in general do not require this kind of close-range accessibility to the pedestrian to as great an extent. Hence, except for banks and sometimes estate agents, they are rarely found on major street frontages. They are able to carry on their business quite adequately on lower-value, less accessible land, often to the rear of the main shopping streets. Offices are also segregated from shops in the vertical dimension, according to the principle that the upper floors of buildings are less accessible than the ground floor. It is common therefore to find a multistorey office block with shops occupying its ground floor street frontage. Even on major shopping streets offices may occupy the upper floors, above the shops.

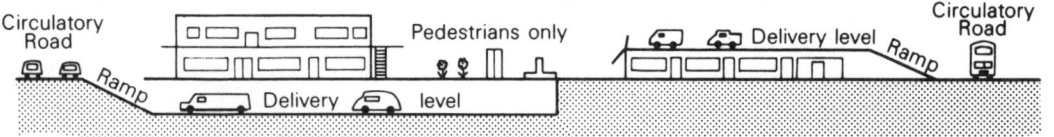

figure 23 Vertical segregation of pedestrians and vehicles

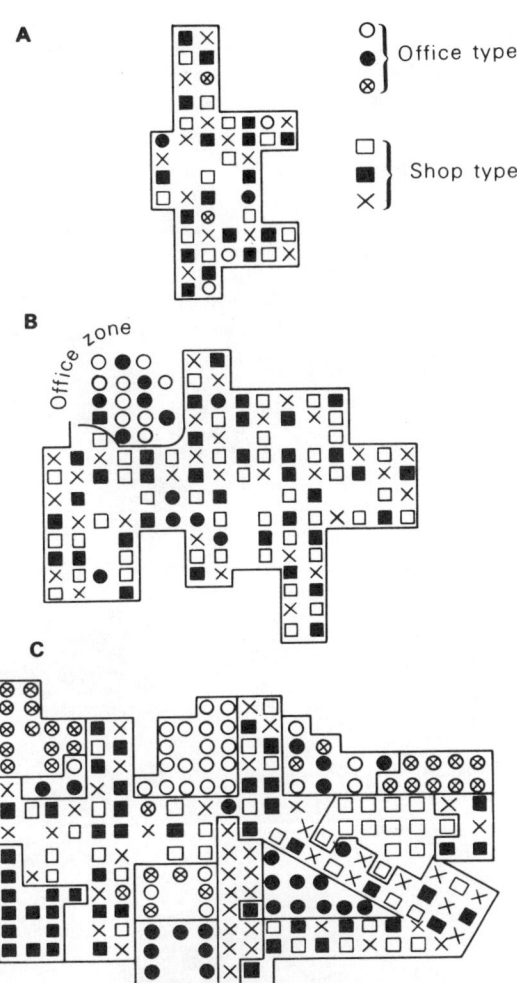

A
○ ●
⊗ } Office types

□
■ } Shop types

B

Office zone

C

figure 24 Land-use in the central business district. A—Small town with no clearly defined zones. B—Larger town with distinct shopping zone and office zone, but no sub-zones. C—large town with shopping and office sub-zones

Manufacturing industries or wholesaling which still exist in the central business district have hardly any need at all for accessibility to the pedestrian. They therefore tend to occupy very inconspicuous sites. Often a fairly large industry of the central business district is the production of the local newspaper. In this case, a central location may be useful to reduce the distances travelled by reporters and delivery vans, but there is very little direct contact with pedestrians.

Residence in the central business district is almost non-existent. Some residents, such as the managers of hotels and clubs may live on the premises, but the density of resident population is extremely low. People who live by choice in the central business district to gain accessibility to theatres and general urban life, often try to arrange that they are able to isolate themselves from the bustle and noise when they wish. They may therefore live in quiet back streets or on the topmost floors of high buildings. It is unlikely that they will wish to locate their residences in close proximity to pedestrian or traffic flows of high volume.

Thus, the functions of the central business district tend to arrange themselves in more or less clearly defined zones which are based largely upon accessibility to pedestrians. The patterns formed by these zones tend to differ according to whether the town in question is large or small. In a small town, with a small central business district, central functions tend to be extremely mixed, and no distinct zones may be recognizable (fig. 24A). This is because, in a very small central business district, there will be little variation in accessibility. With increasing size, a distinct shopping zone soon appears, and then a fairly clear-cut office zone (fig. 24B). With a further increase in size, the friction of distance may begin to operate as walking distances increase. Functions which depend a great deal on one another may then begin to cluster together so as to make contact easier. In other words, urban functions which possess 'linkages' may locate near one another and thus create a set of functional sub-zones (fig. 24C). An area devoted predominantly to shopping may divide up into sub-zones specializing in clothing shops, jewellers and others. Small sub-zones devoted to financial or legal offices may develop within a large office zone. Such sub-zones have developed notably in London where streets such as Oxford Street, Bond Street, Fleet Street, and Whitehall have come to be associated with particular urban functions.

b) Functional linkages

Many central business functions show clear tendencies to locate themselves near other functions with which they have certain links. Department stores and variety stores, sharing the same high-volume pedestrian flow, derive an advantage from clustering, and this is in turn an advantage to shoppers in that it reduces the distance they have to walk to visit the whole group. Most town centres have a cluster of shoe shops, and clothing shops also may show a tendency to cluster. This is because they are selling shopping goods and customers will want to make comparisons between the shops before they buy. An isolated shoe shop would be at a disadvantage because customers would probably decide that they were more likely to obtain satisfaction at a group of shops than at a single shop. Many other types of functional linkages occur. Snack bars near the bus station, hotels near the railway station, restaurants near theatres, legal offices near the courts, banks among leading shops are examples.

It is interesting to make a simple study of the tendency for certain types of shops to be found close together in an actual example of a central business district. Figure 25 is a diagram showing the approximate locations of various types of shops in part of central Gloucester. Table VII shows the extent to which some shop types tend to cluster or to occur near other shop types. It has been constructed in the following way. Eight different shop types have been taken into account (women's clothing, shoes, electrical goods, jewellers, men's clothing, large stores, furniture and supermarkets). The locations of all these shops are indicated by their initial letters in figure 25; the remainder of the shops or offices are labelled O. Each shop of the major types is taken in turn and a count is made of the types of shops which are found next-door and next-door-but-one to it on each side along the shop frontage. Each side of each street or passage is counted separately, and when counting one side of a street no account at all is taken of the shops on the other side. This may cause a slight inaccuracy in some cases, but usually traffic-filled streets are barriers between shops rather than links. If a single shop has two separate frontages, like Woolworth's, British Home Stores and P. Richards in figure 25, it is counted as two shops. Counting is normally conducted along a single shop frontage (e.g. along one side of

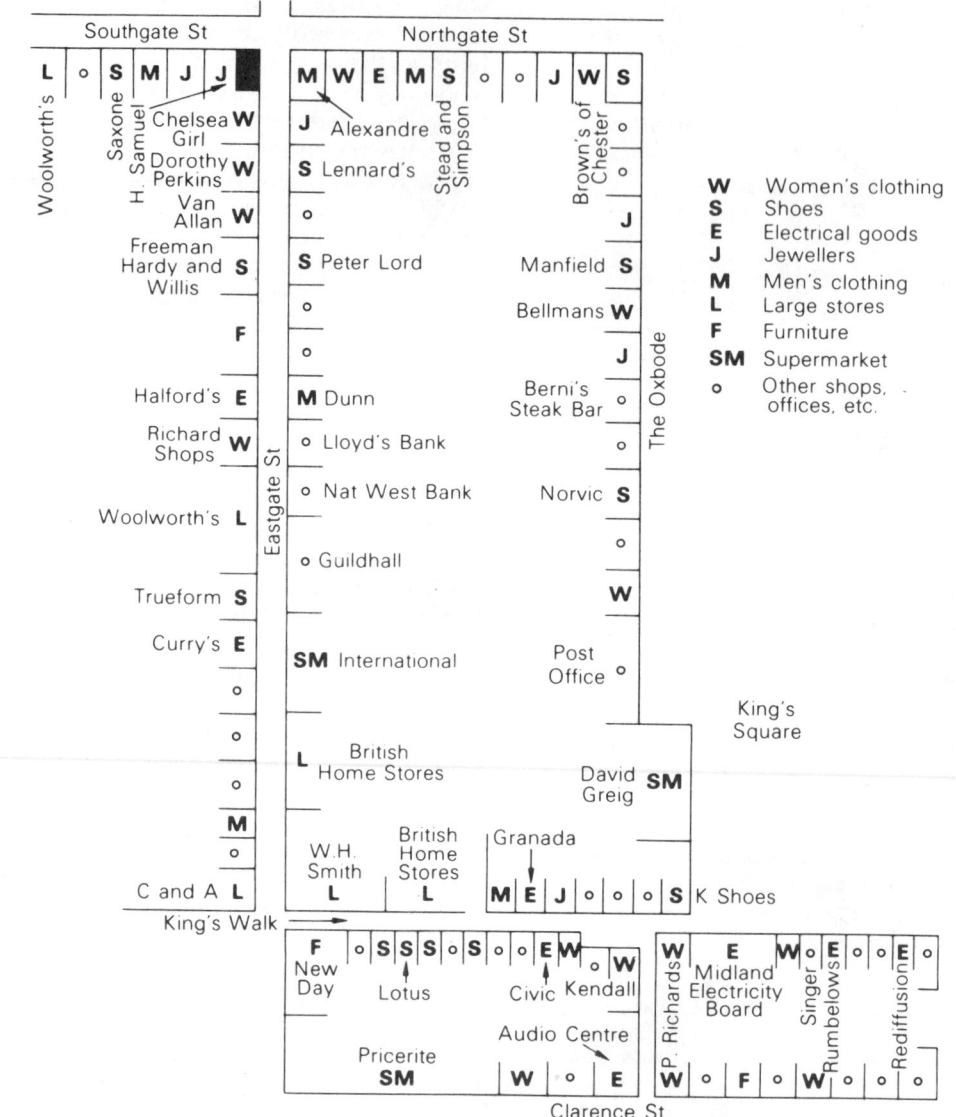

figure 25 Shops of the Eastgate Street area of central Gloucester

W	Women's clothing	
S	Shoes	
E	Electrical goods	
J	Jewellers	
M	Men's clothing	
L	Large stores	
F	Furniture	
SM	Supermarket	
o	Other shops, offices, etc.	

Eastgate Street), but sometimes a shop may have 'neighbours' along more than one frontage. In figure 25, for example, the New Day furniture shop has the following 'neighbours': W. H. Smith and British Home Stores along Eastgate Street, Pricerite and a women's clothing shop into Clarence Street, and an 'other shop' and a shoe shop along King's Walk. Table VII shows that the 15 women's clothing shops have altogether 60 'neighbours', of which the greatest number (apart from 'other shops') are also women's clothing shops (12). But, of course, we might expect this by pure chance even if there were no clustering, because there are more women's clothing shops than any other type. Table VIII lists the number and type of 'neighbours' each shop type would have if they occurred in proportion to the total number of each shop type. Thus we see in Table VIII that, if the women's clothing shops' 60 'neighbours' were shared out in proportion to shop numbers, we would expect only 9 of them to be women's clothing shops. It appears therefore that in this area women's clothing shops tend to cluster together. If we compare the two tables, we also see that shoe shops (10, 7.8) and large stores (6, 1.4) also appear to cluster. Women's clothing shops seem to occur near electrical goods shops (9, 5.4), jewellers near women's clothing shops (7, 4.2) and shoe shops (5, 3.9), and supermarkets near large stores (3, 0.7) and there are other examples. Of course, we are not able to arrive at far-reaching conclusions by such a simple method, considering so few shops, but at least some of our observations might have been expected from the ideas set out in this chapter. Perhaps equally interesting results could be obtained in studies of other central business districts.

TABLE VII *'Neighbour' analysis of shop types in central Gloucester—number of 'neighbours'*

'Neighbour'	Shop Type							
	W (15)	S (14)	E (9)	J (7)	M (6)	L (6)	F (3)	SM (3)
Women's Clothing	12	6	9	7	2	1	5	2
Shoes	6	10	3	5	3	2	2	1
Electrical Goods	9	3	0	1	3	3	1	0
Jewellers	7	5	1	2	4	0	0	0
Men's Clothing	2	3	3	4	0	3	0	0
Large Stores	1	2	3	0	3	6	2	3
Furniture	5	2	1	0	0	2	0	1
Supermarket	2	1	0	0	0	3	1	0
Other Shops	16	24	16	9	9	3	3	6
Total 'Neighbours'	60	56	36	28	24	23	14	13

TABLE VIII *'Neighbour' analysis of shop types in central Gloucester—theoretical number of 'neighbours'*

'Neighbour'	Shop Type							
	W (15)	S (14)	E (9)	J (7)	M (6)	L (6)	F (3)	SM (3)
Women's Clothing	9.0	8.4	5.4	4.2	3.6	3.5	2.1	2.0
Shoes	8.4	7.8	5.0	3.9	3.4	3.2	2.0	1.8
Electrical Goods	5.4	5.0	3.2	2.5	2.2	2.1	1.3	1.2
Jewellers	4.2	3.9	2.5	2.0	1.7	1.6	1.0	0.9
Men's Clothing	3.6	3.4	2.2	1.7	1.4	1.4	0.8	0.8
Large Stores	3.6	3.4	2.2	1.7	1.4	1.4	0.8	0.8
Furniture	1.8	1.7	1.1	0.8	0.7	0.7	0.4	0.4
Supermarket	1.8	1.7	1.1	0.8	0.7	0.7	0.4	0.4
Other Shops	22.2	20.7	13.3	10.4	8.9	8.5	5.2	4.8
Total 'Neighbours'	60.0	56.0	36.0	28.0	24.0	23.1	14.0	13.1

Chapter Eight
Industry and Residence

A INDUSTRY

Manufacturing industries of many different kinds are located in towns, but under the general title of 'industry' we shall also include service industries such as warehousing, in which goods of various kinds are collected and stored until they are delivered to manufacturing firms or shops.

It is not easy to classify urban industries according to their location, but in this chapter we shall classify them in relation to what appears to be the chief factor influencing their location. We shall recognize one group of industries which appear to benefit from a location near some means of transporting bulky materials, another group in which a central location within the town seems to be important, and a final group which appears to place a special value on the availability of large areas of comparatively cheap land. These will be referred to as 'transport-seeking', 'market-seeking' and 'space-seeking' industries respectively. This classification is not altogether satisfactory since some industries will benefit from all three of these factors. None the less the classification will provide a framework for us to gain understanding of the nature of urban industry.

a) Transport-seeking industries

In some types of industries it is much more difficult to transport the raw material than the finished product. A good example is the production of electricity for consumption in the town. In this industry, coal, a very bulky raw material, has to be transported to the electricity works, whereas the electricity itself is very easily transported to consumers. The location of the electricity station in relation to consumers is therefore of little importance, and in fact many electricity stations are now found in rural areas, well outside the towns they supply. A location near a railway or docks for the transport of coal is much more important, and also much may depend on there being a supply of water for cooling purposes. Electricity stations therefore tend to be located where these raw materials can be supplied fairly easily. Such industries are sometimes called 'weight-losing' industries. Oil refining, timber processing, flour milling and sugar refining are other examples. When they occur in coastal towns they are often called 'port industries'.

b) Market-seeking industries

The main consideration in the location of these types of industries is accessibility to their customers. Warehouses for goods which are later to be sold in shops are good examples. Often the goods they handle are not particularly bulky or difficult to transport, so there is little need for them to be located near railways or docks, and the development of containerized transport has given them a much greater choice of location, since goods can now travel in the same container all the way from the manufacturer to the warehouse. It is an advantage, however, for warehouses to be centrally located among their customers. Shops are to some extent concentrated in the central business district, but they also tend to be scattered throughout the town. It appears therefore that a location near the town centre is of advantage to warehouses.

Other industries with similar locational characteristics include newspaper printing, the baking of bread and cakes, car service and repairs, and the manufacture of light engineering products. Industries such as these are often to be found in an area immediately surrounding the central business district, which has been called the 'transition zone'. This is an area, usually of very untidy appearance which, in British towns, usually separates the central business district from the innermost residential zone. One commonly sees a large number of relatively small industrial concerns, often occupying buildings which originally had a completely different use. A great deal of demolition is usually taking place, and open spaces may be used temporarily as rough-and-ready car parks. Generally urban functions are able to change more quickly than the physical structure of the town, so new uses occupy old buildings. In some parts of the transition zone, demolition of old property may be complete and the area may have been re-developed as a new industrial estate, common-ly dominated by warehouses and small engineering works. Despite its untidy appear-ance, the transition zone may be of particular importance in the development of the town's industries since small businessmen are able to obtain relatively cheap accommodation there, and set up quite small firms which may later develop and become considerable em-ployers of labour. An advantage possessed for industry by this inner area of the town is that it is situated quite close to the most densely populated part of the town, and is therefore able to draw upon a conveniently close labour supply. The development of urban motorways and inner ring roads has often provided the industries of the transition zone with easy transport routes to other parts of the town and to other towns.

c) Space-seeking industries

Various kinds of mass-production industries, using 'continuous-flow' methods of manu-facture, need to occupy factories with a very large floor space, so that the different manu-facturing processes can be carried out on a single level, and the products can be moved easily from process to process during manu-facture. Factories of such size are difficult to accommodate in the centres of towns, partly because the urban texture here is so fine-grained (Chapter Four) and partly because

land values are so high (page 29). They there-fore tend to occupy sites near the town's out-skirts where land values are lower and traffic congestion is less severe. Typical industries of the outer areas of towns are food processing and the manufacture of electrical goods and vehicles. Such industries usually have to be conducted on a large scale. Some warehouses may occupy sites such as these, particularly if they are handling fairly bulky goods and it is an advantage to use fork-lift trucks in a single-storey building. Often industrial estates are developed in these areas by local urban councils, particularly if good transport facil-ities are available through access to a trunk road or motorway.

figure 26 Distribution of industry in Vancouver in 1972

d) Industry in Vancouver

Figure 26 shows the general distribution of industry in the city of Vancouver, according to the amount of space which it occupies in each census tract. Even at this generalized scale, it is easy to identify the Burrard Water-front and Marine Drive areas, where sea transport facilities are available. Here, trans-port-seeking industries such as timber pro-cessing and fish packing are of particular importance. Industries in the False Creek Flats area also have the advantage of bulk transport facilities because here are the rail-way yards giving access to eastern Canada and the United States. Market-seeking indus-tries, particularly wholesaling, tend to be

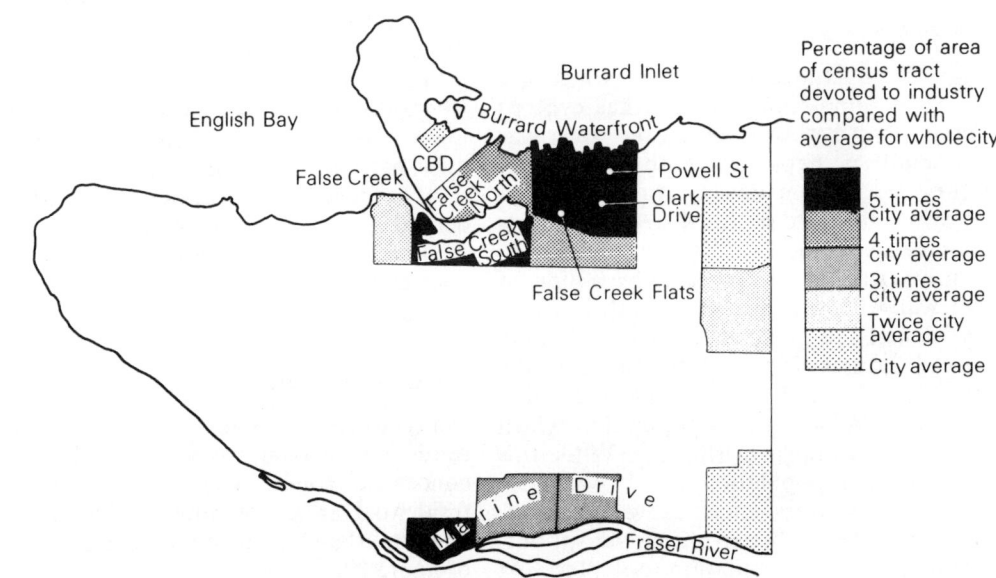

concentrated in the areas immediately south and east of the central business district, supplying markets in central Vancouver and other parts of the Greater Vancouver area.

B RESIDENCE

A great deal of the area of a town is used for the function of residence. People's homes generally seem to occupy the spaces left between the various business and industrial areas. But the residential areas of a town vary greatly in their character, partly as a result of the types of houses and partly through differences in population density and other characteristics of the families which occupy the houses.

a) Population density

Figure 27 illustrates the way in which the pattern of population densities has evolved in many British towns. When the town was very small, perhaps before the nineteenth century, population density was greatest at the town centre and declined steeply towards the outskirts. Sometimes, in fact, the edge of the town was clearly marked by a line of town walls. During the nineteenth century, very densely populated areas of mainly terraced houses were created beyond the margin of the early town. This created a 'wave' of relatively dense population which slowly moved outwards (fig. 27). While this was happening, population density was tending to decrease in the ancient town centre as, beginning with the better-off people, an outward migration of population took place. At

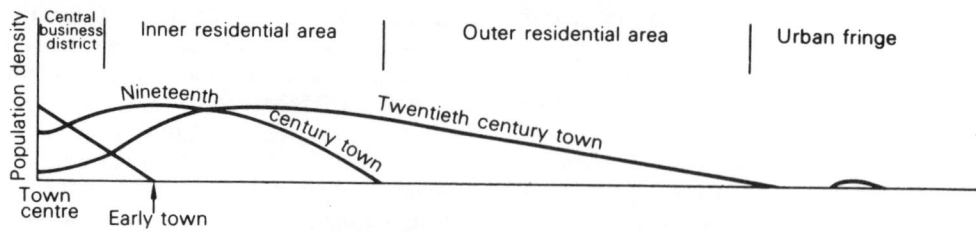

figure 27 Changing urban population densities in British towns

the same time, business activities were beginning to concentrate in the town centre to create the central business district.

The development of the central business district has continued in the twentieth century, and its resident population has become very small indeed. On the other hand, residential development at low densities has caused a great expansion of the town, forming areas where the density of population is generally lower than in the inner districts. In the outermost parts of the town, where urban expansion is encroaching upon farmland, residential areas may be well scattered and separated from one another by fields, golf courses and woodland, thus giving a very low average population density.

b) Residential areas

Many towns seem to possess three major residential areas, arranged in broadly circular, concentric zones. These areas, the inner residential area, the outer residential area, and the urban fringe, are indicated at the top of figure 27.

1 The Inner Residential Area

This district, with its very fine-grained building and street textures, was originally built up in the nineteenth century, and its existence causes many planning problems. Population densities are still very high and there are few open spaces of any size. Many houses are at least a hundred years old and they are often thought to provide inadequate living conditions for the late twentieth century. The area was laid out either before the invention of the motor car or when few people owned cars. As a result hardly any parking facilities are available, and cars have to be left at the kerbside during the night and for much of the day.

Land values in general are relatively high, because of the area's central location but, in contrast, house values are comparatively low. This seems like a contradiction. The explanation is that large numbers of low-value houses are crowded into small areas of valuable land. Average family incomes in this area are usually lower than elsewhere in the town, but families save transport costs because it is only a short distance to the central business district and the inner industrial areas where many people work.

In most towns, the inner residential area is being redeveloped (urban renewal). Older houses are being demolished and replaced either by high-rise flats or new estates in which population density is much lower than before.

2 The Outer Residential Area

In this area, created during the twentieth century, urban physical texture is much coarser. Houses are usually much larger and there is more open space, both public (e.g. school and hospital grounds) and private (e.g. gardens attached to houses). Average family incomes are generally higher than in the inner area. It may seem a little strange that people with higher incomes should tend to occupy land of relatively low value. The explanation is that families in this area are usually occupying and paying for quite a large area of land. Also, houses in this area are generally more expensive than in the inner districts.

Residents of the outer residential area usually live a considerable distance from their work, so daily travel costs may be considerable. Most people depend a great deal on the motor car for journeys to work and shopping trips, and usually the car is catered for by houses having drives and garages where it can be parked. Commuters from this outer residential area contribute greatly to the congestion of the daily 'rush hours' in most towns.

The area is by no means uniform throughout; it is often possible to recognize sub-areas within it. There appears to be a tendency for

figure 28 The outer residential area of Regina

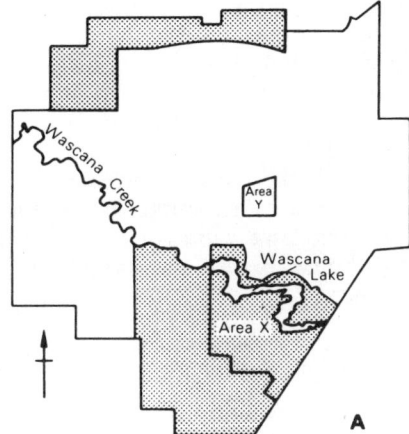

A

Average income per family greater than average for Regina

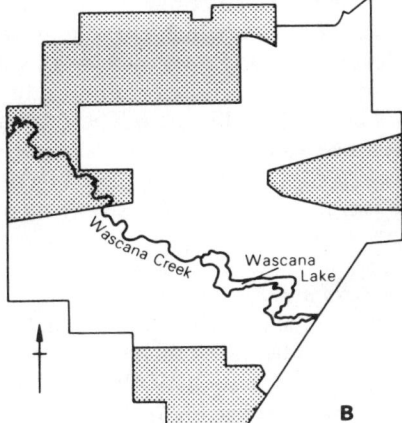

B

Population increase 1966–71 greater than average for Regina

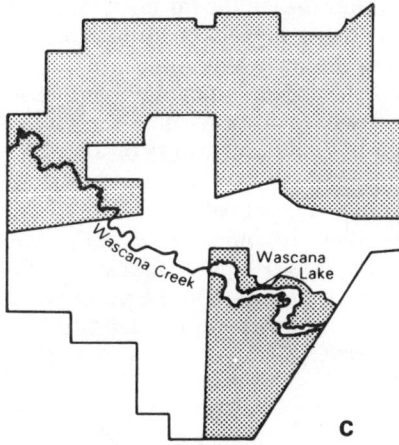

C

Number of children per family greater than average for Regina

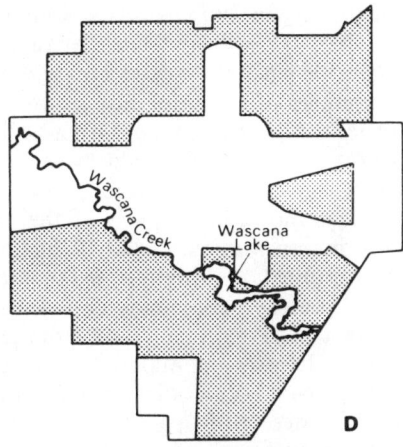

D

More rooms per dwelling than average for Regina

particular districts to be occupied by families of approximately equal income levels. This is not very surprising since new estates are often composed of houses which are sold at similar price levels to people of generally similar income levels. It is also common to find 'council estates' in this area. These began to be developed soon after the First World War, and in some cases may be populated by people who have moved from the decaying inner districts of the town.

3 The Urban Fringe

At its margin the town is expanding into areas of farmland. The value of land for building purposes becomes so high that it becomes unprofitable to use it for farming. Hence, if planning regulations allow, farmers tend to sell their land for the building of houses. This means that open country is gradually encroached upon by the town. Present-day, low-density urban expansion is sometimes called 'urban sprawl', and is often regarded as undesirable since it tends to create monotonous expanses of red-brick houses all of the same general type and shape. Often a Green Belt is created, in which building is strictly controlled, so as to preserve some open country near the built-up parts of the town.

Family incomes in the urban fringe areas may be amongst the highest in the town. Relatively wealthy people may choose to live here in order to gain such advantages as quietness and fresh air, and they may place a special value on scenic sites for their houses, such as hillsides, clifftops or the shores of lakes. In return for these benefits, they may be quite willing to pay very high costs, both in time and money, to travel to work. It is quite common, for example, for London commuters to live in villages in the Sussex downs, and for Manchester commuters to travel daily from homes on the banks of Lake Windermere. Families of the urban fringe live in the 'country' but they are not part of the 'country'; economically and socially they tend to look towards the 'town'.

In general, therefore, from the centre of the town towards its outskirts, population densities and land values tend to decrease, whereas house prices and family incomes tend to increase.

c) Residence in Regina

The four maps in figure 28 illustrate some of the residential characteristics of the city of Regina in the Canadian Prairies. Other Canadian towns and many British towns have similar characteristics. Family incomes are highest (fig. 28A) in the far north and south of the city, rising highest of all in Area X, near Wascana Lake, where they are more than 50 per cent greater than the average for the whole town. In Area Y, near the city centre, average incomes are lowest of all.

Figure 28B shows that population density in the outer districts of Regina is still increasing as they become more fully built-up. Figure 28C and D suggest that young families are relatively common in the outer residential areas, and that their houses tend to be above average size.

In the twentieth century town it is rare to find residential areas and industrial and commercial areas side by side. Recent urban expansion has created large built-up areas devoted almost entirely to residence. Industrial undertakings, on the other hand, tend to be concentrated in relatively small areas, and much of the town's commercial activity is crowded into the central business district. This means that one of the main features of town life is the daily journey to work, when people from most parts of the town converge upon groups of workplaces. Often journeys of considerable length are made, sometimes by public transport, but very often by car.

THE JOURNEY TO WORK IN THE MANCHESTER AREA

Detailed information about journeys to work is found in the Workplace and Transport Tables of the 1966 Sample Census, which can be seen in many public reference libraries. Our study area is shown in figure 29. It consists of 49 administrative districts in the south-east corner of the old (pre-1974) county of Lancashire, which are now almost all included in the new county of Greater Manchester. The area includes seven county boroughs (Bolton, Bury, Manchester, Oldham, Rochdale, Salford and Wigan) which are the largest towns.

a) The workplaces

Altogether over 1.1 million jobs are provided in this area, well over half of which are concentrated in Manchester, Bolton, Salford and Oldham, the four largest towns. Three-quarters of all available jobs in fact are concentrated in only eleven of the administrative districts. This pattern of workplaces is illustrated in figure 30A which clearly shows a major concentration of employment in Manchester and its near neighbours Salford, Stretford and Urmston, together with a semi-circle of 12 to 15 kilometres radius consisting of the 'old cotton towns'.

b) The Residential Areas

Well over a million of the residents of the study area are engaged in employment. About half of these live in the five largest residential districts (Manchester, Bolton, Salford, Oldham and Rochdale). Residences however are not so concentrated as workplaces since three-quarters of the employed population are spread over the *sixteen* largest residential districts (fig. 30B). There is however a general similarity between figures 30A and 30B. All eleven leading workplace districts (fig. 30A) are included in the sixteen largest residential districts (fig. 30B).

It seems reasonable to expect therefore that many journeys to work will be quite short,

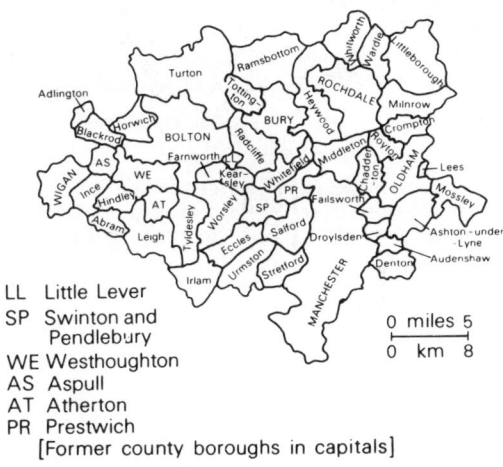

LL   Little Lever
SP   Swinton and
       Pendlebury
WE Westhoughton
AS   Aspull
AT   Atherton
PR   Prestwich
[Former county boroughs in capitals]

figure 29 The Manchester area

both residence and workplace being situated in the same administrative district. In fact, about 65 per cent of the employed population of the whole conurbation work in their home district. This percentage is very much greater in the old industrial towns such as Rochdale (81 per cent), Bolton (80 per cent), Manchester (78 per cent) and Leigh (73 per cent) (fig. 30C). In other districts, notably to the north of Bolton, to the east of Wigan, and to

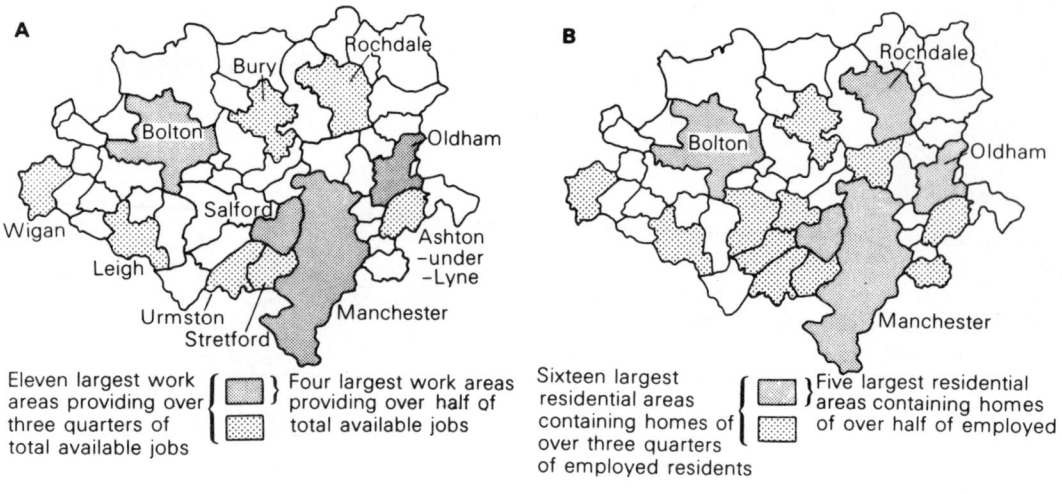

A

Eleven largest work areas providing over three quarters of total available jobs } ▨ { Four largest work areas providing over half of total available jobs ▨

B

Sixteen largest residential areas containing homes of over three quarters of employed residents } ▨ { Five largest residential areas containing homes of over half of employed ▨

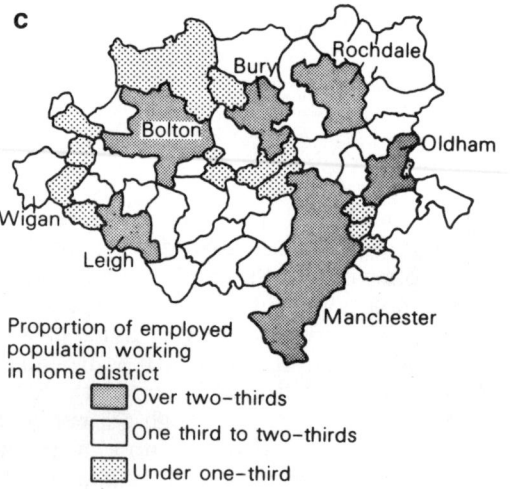

C

Proportion of employed population working in home district

■ Over two–thirds

☐ One third to two–thirds

▨ Under one–third

figure 30

the east and north-west of Manchester (fig. 30c) less than one-third of employed residents work locally. From these areas daily journeys are made to work in the districts where workplaces are concentrated.

c) Recent population changes

Considerable changes in population distribution took place in the Manchester area between 1961 and 1971. In general, population totals declined in the older industrial towns. Manchester and Salford, for example, lost over 15 per cent of their population in ten years. On the other hand, urban expansion invaded rural fringe areas, as shown in figure 31A. Bolton, for example, with a declining population, is almost surrounded by areas where expansion has taken place, including Little Lever, Tottington and Turton, all of which experienced a population increase of over 50 per cent in ten years. A similar area can also be seen to the north of Oldham and to the east of Rochdale. These growing areas still have relatively little industry, so their new residents are obliged to travel to work in established centres of employment.

Figure 31B shows the percentage of households in the various districts which have the use of a car, according to the 1971 Census. There appears to be a similarity between figues 31B and 31A. Areas with a high level of car availability tend generally to have a high rate of population increase. Relatively few households in areas of declining population have the use of a car.

This relationship is illustrated in more detail in Table IX and figure 32.

TABLE IX *Percentage population increase (1961–71) and percentage of households with the use of a car (1971)*

X   Percentage population increase (1961–71)
Y   Percentage of households with the use of a car (1971)

	Rank Order			Rank Order	
	X	*Y*		*X*	*Y*
Bolton	41	41	Irlam	6	16
Bury	22	17	Kearsley	25	26
Manchester	49	46	Lees	16	30
Oldham	44	47	Leigh	34	38
Rochdale	28	39	Littleborough	20	18
Salford	47	49	Little Lever	1	5
Wigan	31	36.5	Middleton	43	33.5
Abram	27	32	Milnrow	9	9.5
Adlington	17	13	Mossley	32	40
Ashton-under-Lyne	39	43.5	Prestwich	40	12
Aspull	21	28	Radcliffe	24	23.5
Atherton	23	31	Ramsbottom	19	6
Audenshaw	37	21	Royton	5	11
Blackrod	8	4	Stretford	45	36.5
Chadderton	35	25	Swinton and		
Crompton	7	9.5	Pendlebury	36	23.5
Denton	14	19	Tottington	2	2
Droylsden	42	35	Turton	3	1
Eccles	46	43.5	Tyldesley	12	15
Failsworth	15	22	Urmston	30	3
Farnworth	38	42	Wardle	18	20
Heywood	10	45	Westhoughton	26	8
Hindley	11	27	Whitefield	4	7
Horwich	33	29	Whitworth	29	33.5
Ince-in-Makerfield	48	48	Worsley	13	14

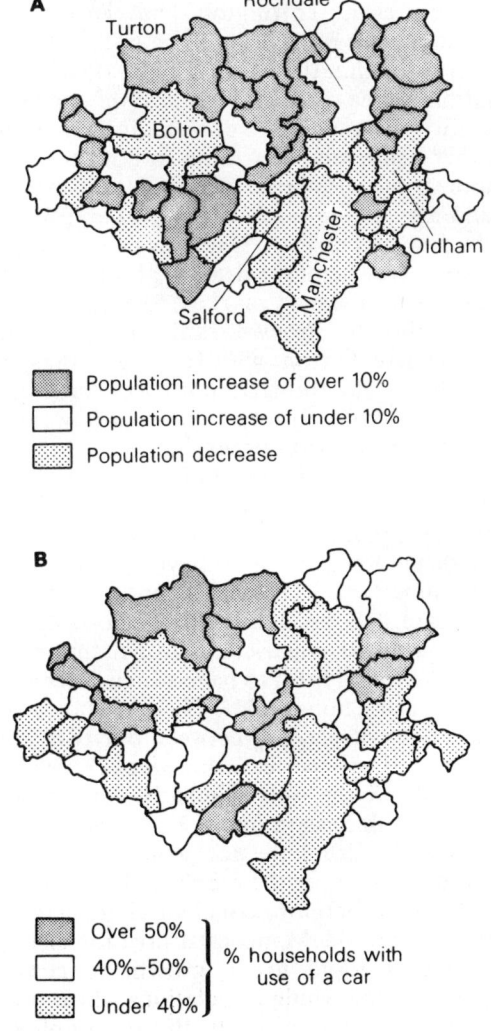

A

Population increase of over 10%
Population increase of under 10%
Population decrease

B

Over 50%
40%–50%   % households with use of a car
Under 40%

figure 31

53

Some points are easy to see in Table IX. Little Lever, Tottington and Turton, for example, are ranked highly in both columns, indicating that they have a high rate of population increase *and* a high level of car availability. Manchester and Salford, on the other hand, have low ranks in both columns, indicating a low rate of population increase and also a low level of car availability. But the rest of Table IX is not so easy to understand. We therefore draw a graph (fig. 32A) on which a dot is marked for each district according to its two ranks in Table IX. Places like Turton, with two high ranks, are plotted in the top-right corner of the graph; places such as Salford, with two low ranks, in the bottom-left corner.

We now see that most of the dots in figure 32A occur in a narrow band on each side of the diagonal line marked. There is a clear tendency for districts to have approximately the same rank in respect of both population increase and car availability. The faster the population of a district has grown, the greater the likelihood for it to have a high percentage of car-using households. There is said to be a 'positive correlation' between our two 'variables'. If a 'perfect' positive correlation existed, all the dots would be placed on a diagonal line, as in figure 32B. If no correlation at all existed, the dots would be scattered haphazardly over the graph, as in figure 32C.

We can therefore conclude that there is a tendency in the Manchester area for districts of recent rapid urban growth to contain mobile, car-owning populations which travel to work in other districts. But the graph also shows a few exceptions to this general rule. Heywood, Hindley and Lees, with rapidly

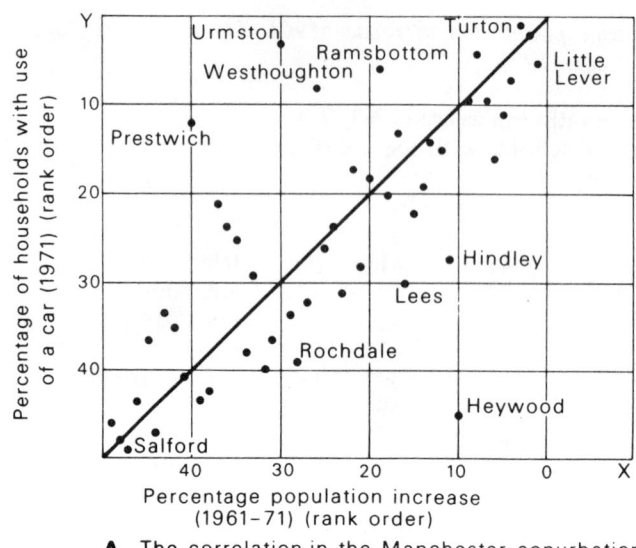

A The correlation in the Manchester conurbation

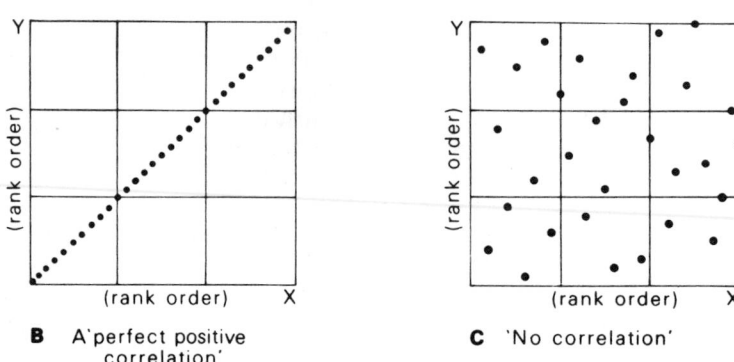

B A 'perfect positive correlation'

C 'No correlation'

figure 32 Plotting the correlation between population increase and car availability

growing populations, have relatively few
households with the use of a car. On the other
hand, Prestwich, Urmston and Westhoughton
have high levels of car availability combined
with a very slow rate of population increase.
Prestwich in fact suffered a decrease of
population between 1961 and 1971.

d) The influence of Manchester as a workplace

One would expect Manchester, as the central
city of the conurbation, and with the largest
number of jobs available, to attract large
numbers of workers from the surrounding
areas. It seems reasonable also to expect that
Manchester will attract a greater proportion
of workers from districts near to it than from
districts farther away.

Figure 33 is a diagram similar to figure 32A.
Droylsden and Prestwich, in the top-right
corner, are very near to Manchester and also
have many residents who work in Manchester.
Wigan, on the other hand, in the bottom-left
corner, has relatively fewer residents making
the much longer journey to work in Manchester. The dots in this diagram are even
closer to the diagonal line than in figure 32A,
indicating that there is an even stronger
positive correlation between the two variables. The diagram makes it quite clear that
there are no outstanding exceptions to the
principle that Manchester's attraction as a
workplace declines as distance from it increases. But we can learn more than this from
figure 33. Districts whose dots are placed
above the diagonal line have a greater proportion of their residents working in Manchester than one would expect in view of the

figure 33

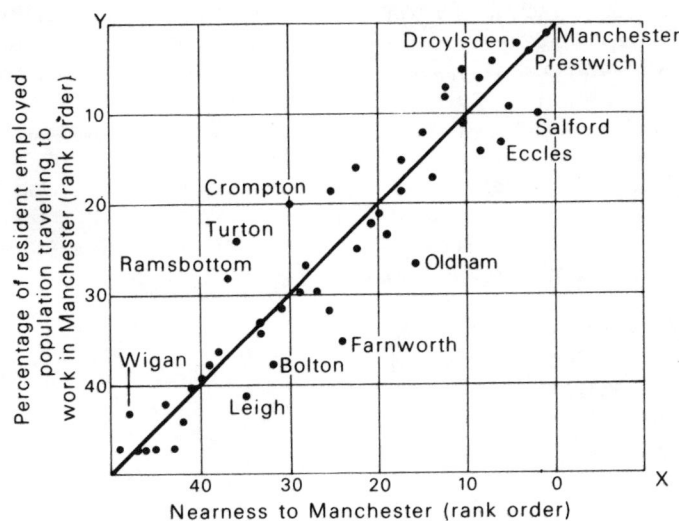

figure 34 Percentage of resident employed population
travelling to work in Manchester

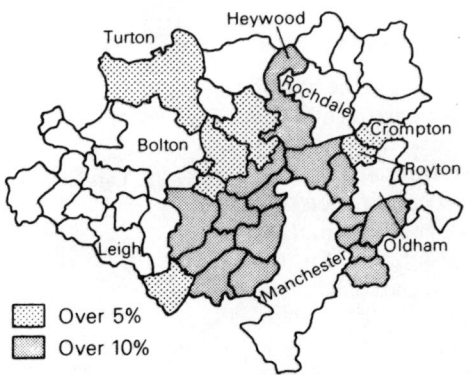

travel distance. Such places include Turton, Ramsbottom and Crompton, to the north of Bolton, Bury and Oldham respectively. These districts have rapidly increasing populations (fig. 31A) and high levels of car availability (fig. 31B). Districts whose dots are placed *below* the diagonal line, such as Leigh, Bolton, Farnworth and Oldham, have fewer residents working in Manchester than we would expect from their location. These are all places with declining populations (fig. 31A) and in which relatively few households have access to a car (fig. 31B). It appears therefore that people who live in recently developed urban areas, where car ownership is relatively high, are more likely to make journeys to work in Manchester.

This suggestion is supported by figure 34 which shows that Manchester has little attraction as a workplace for the residents of old industrial towns such as Leigh, Bolton, Rochdale and Oldham. The influence of Manchester extends in a number of 'tongues' between these towns, tapping districts such as Turton, Heywood, Royton and Crompton.

e) The overall pattern of journeys to work

Figure 35 is an attempt to illustrate the major features of the journey-to-work pattern in the Manchester area. Each arrow on this map represents the largest single outward flow of workers from each district. It can be seen that Manchester is the chief external destination of workers from Bury and Rochdale, though these flows are very small compared with the numbers who find work locally within these towns. Manchester's attraction is particularly

strong immediately east and west of the city, and Salford, despite its considerable size, appears to be dominated by Manchester. Despite their links with Manchester, both Bury and Rochdale succeed in attracting a majority of workers from nearby districts. Bolton, Oldham, Leigh and Wigan are all able to carve out distinct regions, attracting workers radially from surrounding districts.

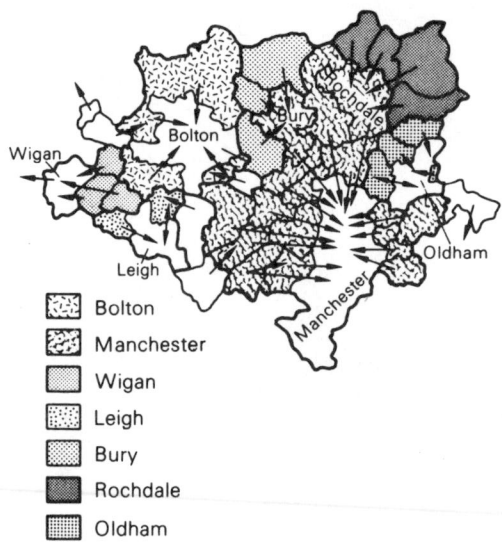

figure 35 Largest single external flow of workers

A THE TOWN AS A SYSTEM

In earlier chapters we have studied the characteristics and locations of shops, offices, industries and residences in urban areas. We have seen that these functions are generally located in buildings in different parts of the town, from the central business district to outlying residential areas. But commercial and industrial premises and areas of housing are not isolated from one another. People and goods need to move from one part of the town to another. People make journeys to work, to school, to shop and to visit friends; goods travel from factories to warehouses, and from warehouses to shops. No part of the town is isolated. Movement takes place in the spaces between the buildings. The town is thus an example of a 'system', in which a large number of buildings devoted to various uses are linked together by channels of movement (mostly roads) which pass through the spaces between them. We can only think of a town as a unit because its different parts are linked together in this way.

Figure 36A shows an imaginary town with a central business district, an industrial area, a school and a small sample of houses. The lines on the diagram show the journeys which residents wish to make each day to go to work and school and to shop. In each case the journey is shown as a straight line (a desire line) going directly from the home to the destination. The diagonal lines are similar desire lines representing through-traffic from a town to the north-east to another town to the south-west, which happen by accident to pass through the town shown. Of course, in making these journeys, it is impossible for people to move in straight lines. Figure 36B shows how these journeys might pass along the town's road network, using the radial roads and the ring road. It is clear that when urban movement is channelled along roads,

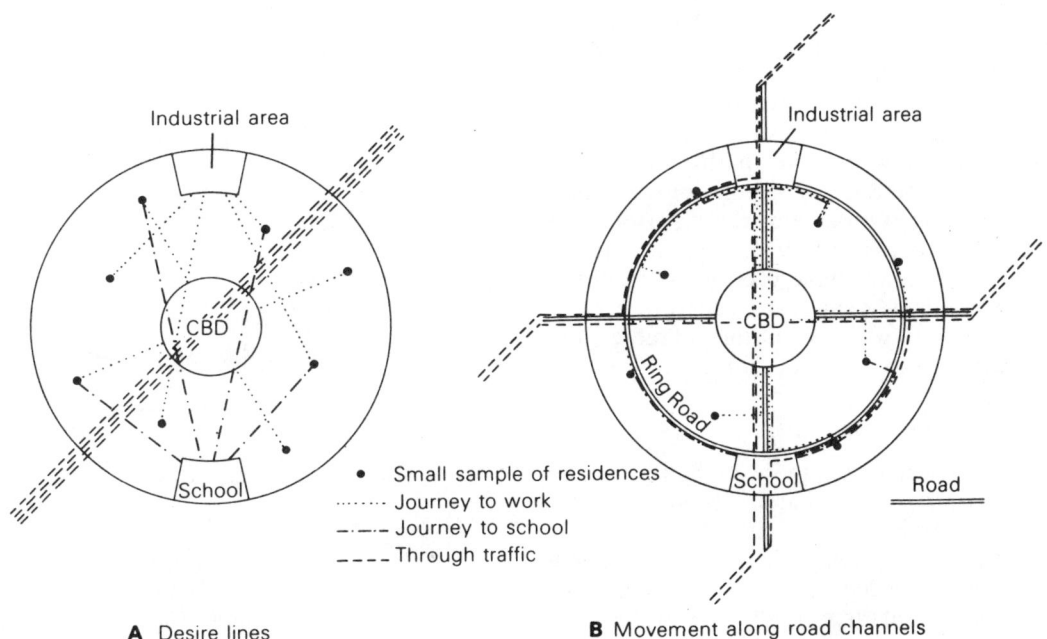

Small sample of residences
.... Journey to work
–·–·– Journey to school
– – – – Through traffic

Road

A Desire lines

B Movement along road channels

figure 36 Movement in a town

traffic may become very heavy on certain stretches of road, and points of traffic congestion may occur, as in the central business district and near the industrial area and the school.

B CONFLICT IN URBAN MOVEMENT

Most road accidents take place in urban areas. This is because urban movement channels are so crowded, and also because they are usually shared between different kinds of traffic, such as cars, vans, lorries, buses, cyclists and pedestrians, all of which travel at different speeds and in a different manner. Car drivers usually wish to travel quickly; buses and delivery vans need to stop from time to time; pedestrians often wish to move at right-angles to the paths of moving vehicles. In places, too, streams of traffic need to cross one another. For these reasons conflicts arise between different types of traffic. Various attempts have been made to reduce these conflicts, usually by separating traffic types in one way or another. Traffic flows more efficiently if it is of a uniform type.

a) Horizontal separation

One way of reducing these conflicts is to allocate certain roads or parts of roads to a single type of traffic.

1 Pedestrians, being the most vulnerable to injury on crowded roads have been provided with pavements free of all other traffic.

2 Traffic moving in one direction along the road is separated from that moving in the

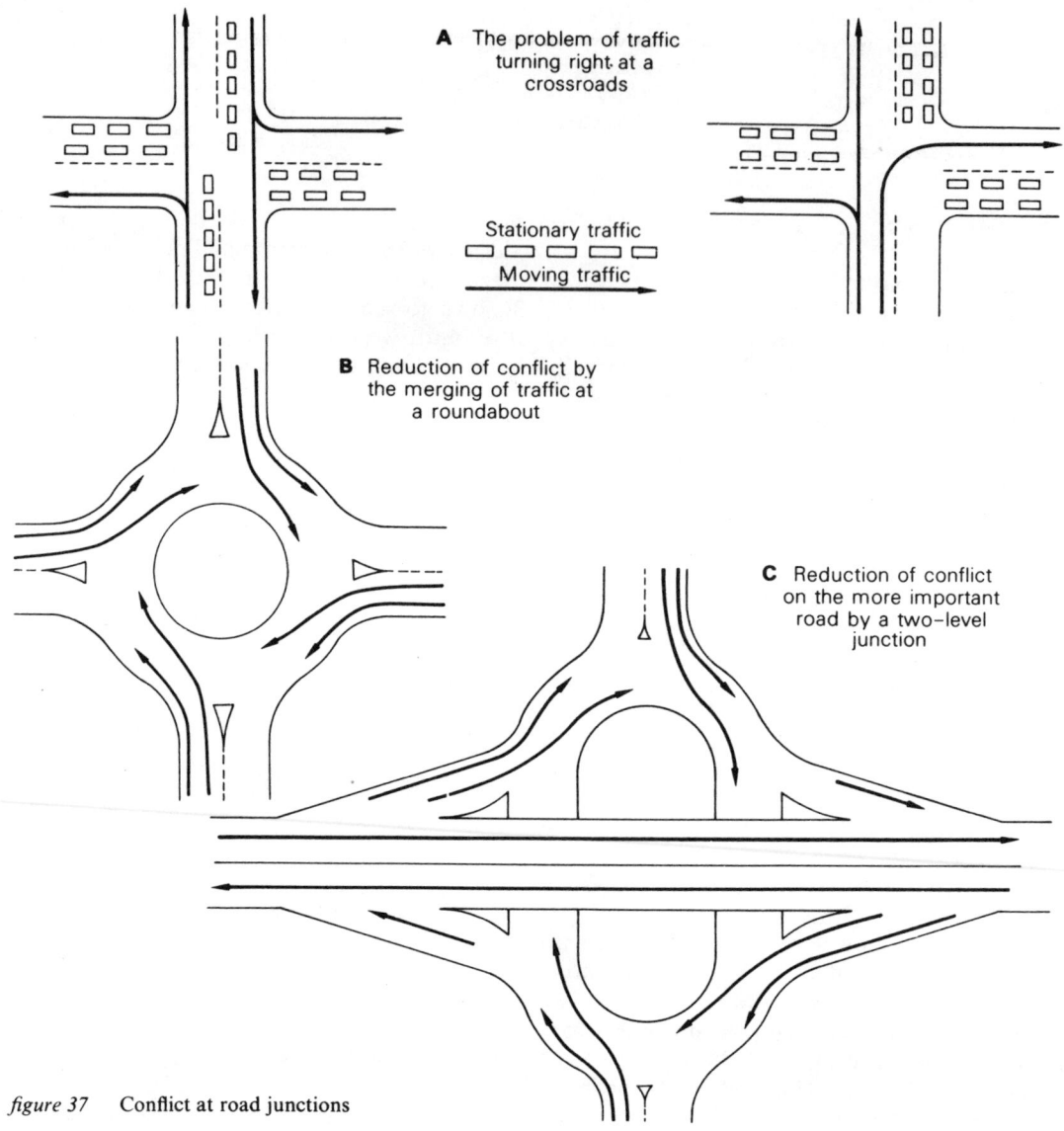

A The problem of traffic turning right at a crossroads

Stationary traffic

Moving traffic

B Reduction of conflict by the merging of traffic at a roundabout

C Reduction of conflict on the more important road by a two-level junction

figure 37   Conflict at road junctions

opposite direction by the 'keep left' principle (in Great Britain). Sometimes a central barrier is erected between the two traffic streams, thus creating a dual-carriageway.

3 Sometimes the whole width of the road is used by traffic moving in the same direction. Since about 1960, many towns have introduced complex one-way systems in their central business districts.

4 In some large cities buses have been given sole use of the kerbside lane of certain busy streets, so that they can stop and start without interference from other vehicles.

5 Because pedestrians need to cross roads they have been given precedence over vehicles at zebra crossings.

b) Vertical separation

Where traffic flows are very heavy, traffic may be separated vertically with each stream at a different level.

1 New movement channels may be created underground, as in the case of the London Underground.

2 Underpasses or bridges may be provided to allow pedestrians to cross busy traffic flows.

3 'Fly-over' junctions (fig. 37C) help to speed traffic, and sometimes a considerable length of road may be elevated, so as to avoid crossing busy ground-level roads.

c) Time separation

Where demand for road space is very intense, arrangements are made for one stream of traffic to have precedence over all others for a short period of time.

1 Pedestrians are provided with pelican crossings, controlled by traffic signals.

2 Busy crossroads have traffic signals giving temporary precedence to one or two traffic streams (fig. 37A). Roundabouts (fig. 37B) tend to reduce conflict between moving vehicles, but at very busy junctions they may have to have traffic signals.

A great problem concerning the planning of urban traffic flows is that the reduction of conflict between types of traffic involves the use of greater amounts of space (fig. 37). In the central areas of cities, where there is the greatest need to reduce conflict, space is very scarce and expensive.

Conflict exists not only between different types of traffic on road channels, but also between motorized traffic and the general quality of life in urban areas. Traffic-filled roads produce noise and fumes which interfere with the pleasure of shopping and even the basic comforts of the home. The building of an urban motorway may help vehicles to move more efficiently, but only at the cost of the discomfort of people who live near it. Many towns have now completely removed traffic from their central shopping areas, and doubts are expressed about the wisdom of building motorways through densely populated residential areas. Good urban planning has to be a compromise between allowing the easy movement of traffic and preserving the quality of the environment.

C THE PLANNING OF THE URBAN ENVIRONMENT

Since the early 1960s a great amount of attention has been paid to the planning of the patterns of buildings and roads in urban

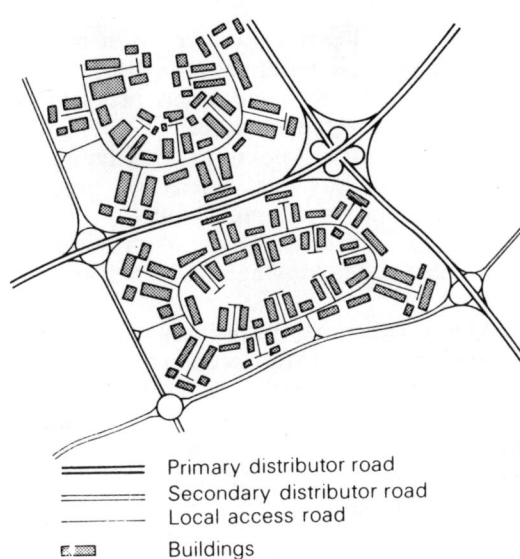

Primary distributor road
Secondary distributor road
Local access road
Buildings

figure 38 Distributor road network and environmental areas

areas. A basic principle has been to attempt to avoid the conflicts described above by linking buildings with roads in such a way that the buildings do not interfere with free movement along the roads, and also that the roads do not destroy the quality of the environment near the buildings. This is a simple principle which we meet every day in school, where the 'activity spaces' (classrooms) are quite separate from the 'movement spaces' (corridors). No part of a school can serve simultaneously as an area of classroom activity and also as a channel of movement.

Figure 38 illustrates an example of this kind of urban planning. Fast, almost conflict-free movement for vehicles is provided by the primary distributor road network. This may consist of dual-carriageway roads of motorway standard. No buildings have direct access to these roads, so there is no problem of vehicles unexpectedly entering or leaving the road. Entry and exit points are very far apart, as on a motorway, and where two primary distributors cross, a complex junction, in this case of the 'clover-leaf' type, is provided so as to keep traffic moving and to reduce conflict.

At intervals along the primary distributors, access is provided to the secondary distributor network by junctions similar to the example illustrated in figure 37c. Again, no buildings have direct access to secondary distributor roads, so as to avoid conflict through roadside parking, but there are a greater number of entry and exit points. Where two secondary distributors cross, a roundabout is provided (fig. 37B). Local access roads are reached by simpler junctions.

Traffic reaches buildings by means of the local access roads, and this network is arranged in such a way that comparatively free movement is always likely to be possible. The great majority of buildings may be reached via a series of cul-de-sacs leading from a circulatory road. It is important that the local access roads should never provide a short cut between different parts of the secondary distributor network. Otherwise heavy through-traffic may begin to use the completely inadequate local access roads. The area served by a particular set of local access roads and bounded by the distributor network has been termed an 'environmental area'. Here the emphasis is upon 'activity' rather than 'movement' and traffic will generally be restricted to local traffic serving

buildings in the local area itself. The environmental area may also be served by cycle tracks and pedestrian ways which cross the primary and secondary distributors by means of bridges or underpasses.

Modifications of this basic principle may be applied to different parts of the town, such as residential areas, industrial estates and the central business district. For example, a circulatory road (of secondary distributor type) may be built completely surrounding the central business district, with car parks on its inner side, from which people may walk to shop in a pedestrian-only precinct without having to cross any traffic flows at all (fig. 39).

To ease access to this road it may be advisable for it to carry only one-way traffic. This also would permit all bus stops to be located on the inner side of the road. Delivery vehicles could leave the circulatory road via ramps to supply shops from roof-top or below-ground levels (fig. 23, p. 42). Figure 39 illustrates an example of this kind of arrangement.

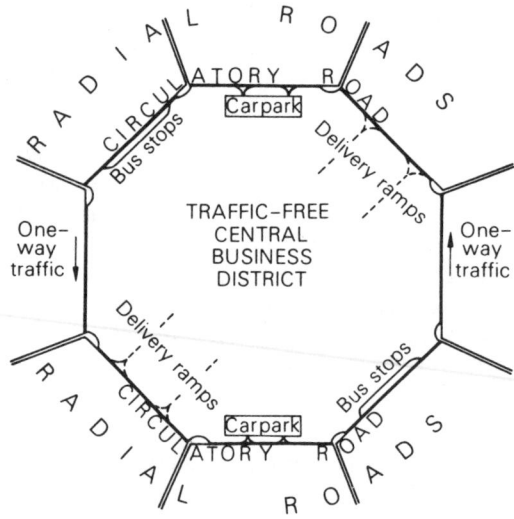

figure 39 The central business district as an environmental area